THE BEATLES IN LIVERPOOL

THE BEATLES IN LIVERPOOL

THE STORIES, THE SCENE, AND THE PATH TO STARDOM

SPENCER LEIGH

OMNIBUS PRESS

Copyright © Elephant Book Company Limited 2012

Published by Omnibus Press
(A Division of Music Sales Limited)

ISBN 978-1-78038-400-9

5 4 3 2 1

Editorial director: Will Steeds
Project manager and picture research: Jane M. Struthers
Liverpool photography by Jeremy Baile and Glen Pearson
Book design: Duncan Youel at Oil Often
Cover design: Oil Often
Retouching, color work and print preparation: Duncan Youel

Printed in China

Note: Roughly speaking, the exchange rate during this period was $3 to £1. The British currency then was pounds (£), shillings (s), and pence (d). There were 20 shillings to a pound and 12 pennies to a shilling.

Front cover: (clockwise from top left) "Love Me Do"—the Beatles' first Parlophone single released in October 1962; the Beatles' first gig in the south of Britain in 1961, organized by Liverpool impresario, Sam Leach; the Beatles acknowledge the Royal box at the end of their set in the Royal Command Performance at the Prince of Wales Theatre, 1963; setting the fashion trends with their famous collarless suits; the boys in their hometown of Liverpool, February 19, 1963.
Back cover: (left) the front of a fan club card produced for the "Beatles for their Fans" night at the Cavern, April 5, 1962; (right) the Beatles pose for an early group portrait, 1962.
Facing title page: The Beatles (left to right) Ringo Starr, John Lennon, Paul McCartney, and George Harrison, 1962.

CONTENTS

BEATLE CITY

"We see in papers all over the world—isn't it wonderful that the Beatles rose from the slums. Lots of people imagine that Liverpool is one big slum, which it isn't."

JOHN LENNON, 1964

IN FEBRUARY 2012, LIVERPOOL CITY COUNCIL ANNOUNCED A YEAR OF BEATLE CELEBRATIONS—JUST LIKE ANY OTHER YEAR, YOU MIGHT THINK—but this year was special, marking the fiftieth anniversary of Ringo Starr's joining the Beatles and the release of their first Parlophone single, "Love Me Do." "What we have in Liverpool," comments Dave Jones, the Cavern Club's co-owner, "the rest of the world would die for." And it's true. In 1962, Liverpool had a significant but declining port in northwest England, and in spite of the city's poverty it had a feisty community spirit, especially in working class areas. Indeed, there was even pride that the football pools—a working class passion in pre-lottery days—was run from Liverpool by Littlewoods and Vernons. Although there was no passion for football among the Beatles themselves, we now know that John Lennon was a Red (Liverpool FC) and Paul McCartney a Blue (Everton FC).

Situated on the River Mersey, Liverpool's port looked west toward Ireland—and America. The city's inhabitants felt special about this unique international relationship, which had begun following the founding of Liverpool by King John in 1207. At that time, the English had recently conquered Ireland, and Liverpool's harbor was in a perfect location for sending supplies and trade across the Irish Sea. Ireland remained Liverpool's main trading partner into the sixteenth century, and the town became a hub for merchants and tradesmen. By the seventeenth and eighteenth centuries, Liverpool was experiencing an economic boom. Daniel Defoe, the author of *Robinson Crusoe* and something of an eighteenth-century Bill Bryson, wrote, "Liverpool has an opulent, flourishing and increasing trade to Virginia, and the English island colonies in America. They trade round the whole island, send ships to Norway, to Hamburg, and to the Baltic, as also to Holland and Flanders; so they are almost like Londoners, universal merchants." Evidence of Liverpool's wealth resonates today in the magnificent architecture throughout the city.

As the port became central to trade routes across the Atlantic to America and the West Indies, Liverpool became one of the largest slave ports in the Atlantic Slave Trade, thereby eclipsing Bristol and London as Britain's leading port. Supplies from Manchester were used to trade with Africans in return for their slaves. In turn, slaves were transported across the Atlantic to the West Indies, and sugar was brought back to Liverpool. Many merchants made huge profits from the slave trade until the practice was declared illegal and abolished in 1807. Following its abolition there were concerns that Liverpool's success would decline, but in fact the port continued to flourish, and shipbuilding became as successful as trade.

The town's port had already benefitted the surrounding areas of Lancashire and Manchester, which were strongholds of the textile industry; to cope with the demand, transport links from the port to neighboring areas were vital. In 1830, the Manchester-to-Liverpool railway opened, improving the speed and distribution of commodities and people; construction of the world's first electrically operated overhead railway, which stretched the eight miles of Liverpool's dockland, was completed in 1893. (Unfortunately, the railway closed in 1956 and was demolished.) Liverpool's borders continued to expand to accommodate the growth in population caused by migration into the city from other areas in Britain and from

overseas, in particular from Ireland following the famine of 1846–48. In 1880, Liverpool was officially granted city status.

As well as trade, the city promoted commercial passenger liners. Cunard operated a direct route from Liverpool to New York, and its merchant seamen became known as Cunard Yanks. Three buildings on the waterfront—housing Cunard, the Port of Liverpool, and Royal Liver (an insurance company)—are known as the Three Graces. All opened in the early twentieth century, and fortunately all still stand today, even though Liverpool became a main target for Hitler during World War II. The fierce and continual bombing took an enormous toll on the city's population and its streets and buildings. The city could not afford to repair all the bomb damage, and neglected sites were still being used as makeshift playgrounds in the early 1960s. Although the photographs of the Beatles leaping for joy on wasteland, taken for the "Twist and Shout" EP, were shot in London, the cover was actually making a point about their home city— even the façades of magnificent buildings such as St. George's Hall or the Royal Liver Building were dirty and grimy.

During the war, American servicemen were stationed on Merseyside, and Liverpool's youth, as well as the United Kingdom in general, had an interest in American popular culture—their movies, music, cameras, fashions (nylon stockings, in particular), and junk food (popcorn and hamburgers). Postwar austerity remained—rationing did not end until 1954—but the Cunard Yanks would continue to return home with the latest American fashions; I know one Cunard Yank who even took a refrigerator through customs without being stopped.

There is, however, still much debate as to how influential the Cunard Yanks were on the local music scene. Certainly those who had relatives in the States or on the ships may have had access to the music from America, but as the Cavern's DJ, Bob

Top left: The iconic Royal Liver Building on Liverpool's waterfront. Opened in 1911, it was the home of the Royal Liver Assurance Group.
Bottom left: Symbols of Liverpool's maritime past, the Three Graces: the Royal Liver Building, Cunard Building, and Port of Liverpool Building located on the waterfront at Pier Head.

Wooler, said, "I accept that there were hundreds of Cunard Yanks and that, before the war, they brought back dance band records, which were unavailable here. And in the 1950s they brought back country and western records, which were not released here. However, there is no evidence that the beat groups were performing songs that were brought over from America by the Cunard Yanks." Over three hundred songs were covered on records by the Liverpool bands; every one of those originals was released in the UK, and hence would have been available at NEMS (North End Music Stores). Furthermore, in all my interviews with Liverpool musicians, I have never come across anyone who has acknowledged the Cunard Yanks as a source for obtaining their music. Sorry, fellas.

By the 1970s and '80s Britain was in recession, and Liverpool was suffering from high unemployment. The release of UK cabinet papers in 2011 showed that the Tory government under Mrs. Thatcher was considering "managed decline" for the city. Air travel for passengers and freight as well as increased competition in cargo shipping had also contributed to the downsizing of the docks. Fortunately, a minister for Merseyside was created, and the docks started to expand again when the city recast itself as a container port.

There is much rebuilding and development that could, and should, be done in Liverpool, but with a parlous economy it is unlikely that much will happen for many years. Still, Liverpool is in a stronger position to face the future than many cities. The reason can be explained in one word: tourism. And the reason for that tourism can be explained in another: Beatles. Liverpool's future relies on its past.

LIVERPOOL'S BOYS

Today, Liverpool is firmly established on the tourist map, and tourists will continue to visit, just as they travel to Memphis for Elvis, to Stratford-upon-Avon for Shakespeare, and to Salzburg for Mozart. Admittedly, the music of some earlier icons—such as Ivor Novello and Noël Coward—has become unfashionable, but this is unlikely to happen to the Beatles. Their story is magical, and tourists will always want to see

Above: Liverpool docks in the 1950s.
Below: The world's first electric elevated railway, constructed in 1893. The dockers walked underneath the railway to protect them from the rain, and so it became known locally as the Dockers' Umbrella.

the buildings and the streets associated with them. Their infectious music has been performed and sampled in so many different ways that it remains fresh and contemporary for future generations to discover.

Prior to the Beatles, most British pop stars were local substitutes for the American variety. The Beatles paraded their upbringing with pride, and growing up in Liverpool

was crucial to their development. Some commentators call Liverpool the fifth Beatle. This connection is highly significant. The very unity of the Beatles would have been broken if one of them had come from, say, nearby Warrington or the Wirral peninsula instead of Liverpool. As they were all war babies, it is a quirk of fate that not one of their mothers went to a safe haven in North Wales to give birth.

The Beatles were born and raised in Liverpool, and so, by definition, they are Scousers. In the nineteenth century, scouse was a cheap stew made from leftovers; the term also refers to the Liverpool accent, a hybrid developed from the Welsh and Irish who came to live in the dock city, plus a little catarrh. Because the Beatles' accent sounded friendly, their manager, Brian Epstein, encouraged them not to change it. Another of his protégés, Cilla Black, had an especially pronounced Scouse accent.

The Beatles' accent contributed to their depiction as working class heroes. "Wasn't the image generally, outside of Liverpool, that Liverpudlians were all downtrodden and ill-educated and ill-fed and everything else?" says their press officer, Tony Barrow. "The Beatles had a working class image for no good reason at all, except that they came from Liverpool."

It now seems incredible that the city denied its Beatle heritage during the 1970s, but once residents of the same generation as the Beatles became councilors, recognition of the band's legacy and tributes to them started to take shape. It is both cynical and accurate to say that the assassination of John Lennon in December 1980 kick-started the city's celebration of its most famous son.

However, John Lennon's death has skewed our view of the Beatles. Over half of the tourists cite John as their favorite Beatle, based on their impression that it was his group. Initially it was, but anyone who grew up in the 1960s will know that it was equally John's and Paul's group, and it seems to irk Paul that he is now seen as second-ranked. There is nothing he can do about it. John's assassination did rewrite history; indeed, Paul, in an unguarded moment, confided to Hunter Davies that he couldn't compete with "Saint John"—

Above: This is one of a sequence of photographs taken in Liverpool by the London photographer Michael Ward on February 19, 1963—the day that "Please Please Me" had reached the top of the *New Musical Express* charts.

and Paul, more than anyone, knew that John had his faults.

Although the effect was unintended, the sheer power of John and Paul's personalities and their songwriting kept George Harrison on the sidelines. You can sense George's frustration in Martin Scorsese's superb 2011 documentary *Living in the Material World*—and, incidentally, note how favorably Paul speaks of George. He likens the Beatles to the four corners of a square; such a generous comparison would not have been made in the '60s.

Remarkably, there are still those in Liverpool who deny the Beatles' impact on and importance to the city, but they are fewer now than in the past. These skeptics call in to radio shows and ask, "What did the Beatles ever do for Liverpool?" The answer is a heck of a lot, but even if they hadn't, it was enough that they were born there.

Welcome, then, to the story of the Beatles in Liverpool. The story is largely told chronologically, and I have tried to write it without hindsight. In 1962, the Beatles did not know what would happen to them; it should be the same for readers. No matter what we may think, the Beatles' success was by no means inevitable.

LIVERPOOL VOICES

Liverpool, as everyone knows, is a city of entertainment. Even prior to the '60s, popular singers (Lita Roza, Frankie Vaughan, Russ Hamilton) and comedians (Tommy Handley, Arthur Askey, Ted Ray, Ken Dodd) came from the city. In the early '60s everything exploded with the advent of Merseybeat, with over three hundred groups performing in the city and its suburbs. To compete, many country musicians added a beat to their music, and for a time Liverpool was known as the Nashville of England.

"I have met people from Birmingham and Manchester and not known for a couple of years where they have come from, but Liverpudlians let you know at once."

GEORGE MELLY, JAZZ SINGER

"Before I came to England, people were telling me how reserved the English were. Then I came to Liverpool and found the Scousers were fantastic. They remind me of the midwest: good hard-working people who love to be entertained and love music and want to have fun. Anyone who says the English are reserved hasn't been to Liverpool."

RAUL MALO, MAVERICKS

"Scousers have got to sing. Scousers have got to have music."

MICK O'TOOLE, IN THE MOVIE THAT HONKY TONK SPIRIT (2011)

"If you were asked to choose somewhere to be brought up, you would pick somewhere else, but I was told I was lucky. You're lucky to be born in Liverpool; you're lucky to be born a Catholic; you're lucky to be born short-sighted; and you're lucky to be born during the Blitz."

ROGER McGOUGH, POET AND MEMBER OF SCAFFOLD

Top, left: George Melly with Mick Mulligan (on trumpet) and his Magnolia Jazz Band, 1961.
Left: Roger McGough, member of Scaffold, 1967.

"One time we did a show and John Lennon said, 'I don't go much on your music, son, but give us your hat.' I told him that I didn't think much of his music, come to that, and I didn't think that they would get anywhere unless they got with it and played country."

THE HILLBILLY DOCKER, HANK WALTERS

"My father used to say to me, 'Sing out. Don't do this "ba-ba-ba-booing" like Bing Crosby.' I got used to doing big-voiced things."

KEN DODD, LIVERPOOL COMEDIAN AND BALLAD SINGER

"I have a lot to thank the city for—I think my voice can be attributed to a good pair of lungs and the Liverpool air."

LITA ROZA, 1950s HITMAKER FROM LIVERPOOL

"The Beatles transformed everything, including Liverpool. Liverpool might not have become the amazing modern city that it has become without them. I came here in the '70s and Liverpool was not a place where you went walking late at night. It was criminally infested, and now there is something magical going on. The Swiss psychiatrist Carl Jung called it the Pool of Life, and he was right."

MICK ROCK, ROCK PHOTOGRAPHER

Top: A 1959 booking card advertising Hank Walters and the Dusty Road Ramblers, billed as "Liverpool's Top Country & Western Group."
Above: Born in Knotty Ash, Liverpool, in 1927, comedian Ken Dodd was one of the most successful recording artists of the 1960s. In 1965 his song "Tears" topped the UK charts for five weeks. It sold over a million copies, making it the UK's biggest selling single by a solo artist that year.

11

1 GROWING UP IN LIVERPOOL

"Non nobis solum sed toti mundo nati. (Not for ourselves alone but for the good of the world.)"

SCHOOL MOTTO, LIVERPOOL INSTITUTE

"Quarrymen, Quarrymen, Strong before our birth."

QUARRY BANK SCHOOL SONG

Left: One of the series of photographs taken by Michael Ward. The Beatles are on the steps at Liverpool docks with cups of tea bought from a nearby stall.

ANYONE LISTENING TO JOHN LENNON'S 1970 SONG "Working Class Hero" might assume that he had had an underprivileged, unpleasant childhood. This is far from the truth. Visiting his childhood home in the leafy Woolton suburb, you would never think of him as working class. Ringo is really the only Beatle to whom the label "working class" would apply. But despite the poverty in the city during the Beatles' childhoods, there was a general sense of community, especially in the working class areas around Scotland Road, the home of fellow Liverpudlian singers Frankie Vaughan and Cilla Black. Of course, you can argue over the meaning of Lennon's lyric—does a working class hero have to be working class himself?

John was the son of Alfred Lennon, known as Freddie, who was born in Liverpool on December 14, 1912. In 1927, Freddie met fourteen-year-old Julia Stanley in the Liverpool district of Sefton Park. They had a long courtship, partly because they were so young and partly because he worked as a ship's steward. They were married at the Mount Pleasant Registry Office in 1938, and the next day Freddie left on a three-month voyage to the West Indies. Due to Freddie's work, they were to see little of each other during their married life.

Britain declared war on Germany in September 1939, and the Germans launched air attacks on port cities. The unfortunate residents around the Liverpool docks found their streets reduced to rubble. From August 1940 to May 1941 there was a Blitz on Liverpool, with over 7,000 people killed or seriously injured and 120,000 homes damaged or destroyed. Nobody knew when the devastation would end or indeed whether Britain would even be victorious.

At a mass burial in the city, several of the bodies were unidentified and placed in a common grave. The bishop of Liverpool, searching for the right words, said that God would know them, and that's all that really mattered. In November 1940, before Billy Kinsley of the Merseybeats was born, seven members of his family were killed in a single bombing raid. An official report into the bombing blitz on Merseyside concluded, "Measured by the weight and number

Top: The destruction caused by WWII bombing. This view is from the Tower Buildings located on the Strand, opposite the Royal Liver Building, and was photographed after the Blitz in August 1941.
Above: John's first home in Newcastle Road, Wavertree. The house was his mother's parents' home.
Opposite, top: Dovedale Primary School class of 1947. The students pose in front of the brick-built air-raid shelter. John is in the back row, eighth from the left.
Opposite center and bottom: Views of Menlove Avenue.

of attacks, and number of casualties, Merseyside was Hitler's number one target outside London."

John Lennon's Aunt Mimi told a reporter that he was born during an air raid, but this is incorrect; the skies were clear on the night of October 9, 1940. John Winston Lennon (his middle name an acknowledgment of the great wartime leader Winston Churchill) was born at the maternity hospital in Oxford Street while Freddie was at sea. Julia brought John back to her parents' home in Newcastle Road, Wavertree.

The family regarded Freddie as a ne'er-do-well, although he regularly sent money to Julia. He had misadventures on board ship and was jailed for stealing vodka. Freddie wrote a letter (which he later came to regret) suggesting that Julia should enjoy herself by seeing other men. Julia took him at his word. She had an affair with a soldier and gave birth to his child, Victoria, who was adopted by a Norwegian sailor. She then met and lived with John Dykins, a waiter at the Adelphi Hotel. They had two children, John's half-sisters, Julia (born 1947) and Jacqueline (born 1949). Julia is now the director of the Cavern and is often seen at Beatles conventions, but Jacqueline has shunned publicity.

John's mother Julia had a sister, Mary (known as Mimi), a nurse who became a ward sister at Woolton Convalescent Home. Mimi was engaged to a doctor, but he died before they could marry. Following his death, she began a relationship with George Smith, a cheerful man who worked at his family-owned dairy farm and delivered milk to Mimi's home. Once married, they lived in "Mendips," an impressive three-bedroom house at 251 Menlove Avenue, Woolton. Situated next to a tree-lined road and surrounded by countryside, the house was also close to the grounds of the Salvation Army hostel, Strawberry Field (which John would always refer to as "Strawberry Fields"), and George's livestock were less than a mile away. While George was on wartime service, however, his brother Frank sold their land to a stocking factory; on his return from the service, George became the factory's night watchman.

Above: John, in the early 1950s, at the front door of Mendips in Menlove Avenue.
Opposite: Dovedale Primary class of 1951–52. John is in the back row, fifth from the left. His friend Michael Hill (in the striped sweater) is in the next row down at the far right.
Opposite, below: John Lennon, aged 8, with his mother in the back garden at Mendips.

From early childhood John lived with his aunt Mimi at Mendips, so between 1946 and 1952 he attended the nearby Dovedale Road Primary School, off Penny Lane. George Harrison was a pupil there in 1948, but as George was two years younger, John may not have been aware of him at the time.

John's childhood friend, Michael Hill, was in the same class as John at both Dovedale and then Quarry Bank High School. Michael remembers John as a tough kid, "but his fighting changed from physical to verbal as he got older. He had a wonderful command of the English language, and an extraordinary range of swear words. I don't know where he got them from, probably from the older boys 'round the neighborhood."

In the final year of his primary school, John and Michael took the eleven-plus examination (a pass-fail exam that would determine a student's future educational path: grammar school, secondary modern, or technical). Both passed, which enabled them to attend a grammar school, in their case Quarry Bank High School. "Somebody once said to me that I was John Lennon's lieutenant," comments fellow Quarry Bank pupil Pete Shotton, "but that's not the way it was at all; best mates don't have a hierarchy. I always considered myself to be totally equal with John throughout our teenage years and into adulthood."

John and Pete didn't work, but Michael had a part-time job delivering newspapers, so he saved his earnings and bought records. "They seemed to think that I had a magical supply of records from the States," comments Michael, "but they came from the local record shop in Elm Hall Drive."

Thus Michael played a part in fostering John's love of rock 'n' roll; as John didn't have a record player at home, he would spend hours at Michael's house listening to records. "I started off listening to jazz," recalls Michael. "But John wasn't terribly interested in it. And then I got into Hank Williams, which he loved. He also loved 'Caribbean,' by Mitchell Torok, and pop music—Guy Mitchell and Frankie Laine. We also listened to Johnnie Ray, *Live at the Palladium*. When skiffle came along, I had several records by Lonnie Donegan, and we also listened to rock 'n' roll—Bill Haley and Elvis."

During John's studies at Quarry Bank, Mimi's husband, George, died. It would have been an unsettling time, as Aunt Mimi was determined to remain at Menlove Avenue and took in lodgers so she would have enough money to retain the house. In 2007 it came to light that during that time she had had an affair with one of the lodgers, a biochemistry student, Michael Fishwick—a revelation that belied her straitlaced image. It's unlikely that John knew of the affair at the time, but if he had, one can't help feeling he would have said, "Good on you, Mimi."

John didn't fare well in his exams at Quarry Bank. He and Pete were unruly and disruptive and often received the

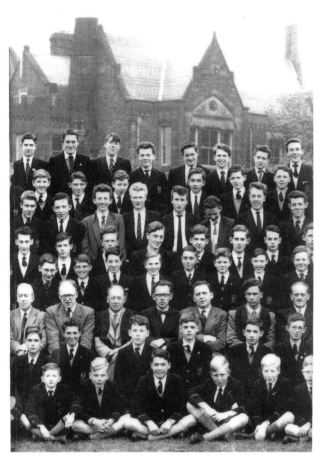

Far Left: Quarry Bank Grammar School photo, 1957 (detail).
Left: William Pobjoy, Quarry Bank's headmaster, who helped John get into Liverpool Art School.
Below, left: Ivan Vaughan, who attended the Liverpool Institute and introduced Paul to John.
Opposite, top and below: John Lennon's submissions to the school magazine—*The Quarry*—illustrating an early love of drawing and wordplay that would continue throughout his life. Top: his cartoon for the Christmas 1956 issue; below: his poem "The Tale of Hermit Fred" featured in the Easter 1957 issue.

cane or detention. They had no interest in studying, and when John took his O-level exams in 1957, he failed them all. Nevertheless, the school's headmaster, William Pobjoy, recognized some potential and secured an interview for him at the Liverpool College of Art. Wearing his Uncle George's suit, John took along some drawings and was accepted.

John lived very close to Pete and two other friends, Nigel Walley and Ivan Vaughan. Ivan attended the Liverpool Institute, and it was he who would later introduce a friend of his to John at St. Peter's church fete. That friend was Paul McCartney.

James Paul McCartney, the first child of Jim and Mary McCartney, was born in Walton Hospital on June 18, 1942. His brother, Mike, was born in 1944. The McCartneys lived at 10 Sunbury Road, Anfield. During the war Jim worked at

a munitions factory; in peacetime he worked as a salesman at the Cotton Exchange. He encouraged Paul to complete the daily crossword in the newspaper, and Paul became the best speller in his class. When he was eleven, he won an interschool prize for his essay on the monarchy to celebrate the coronation of Queen Elizabeth II.

As a domiciliary midwife, Mary McCartney earned more than her husband. She had always wanted to move to better housing, and so, in May 1955, the McCartneys moved to their seventh and most celebrated address—20 Forthlin Road, Allerton. The extended family was a close and loving one, and Paul would one

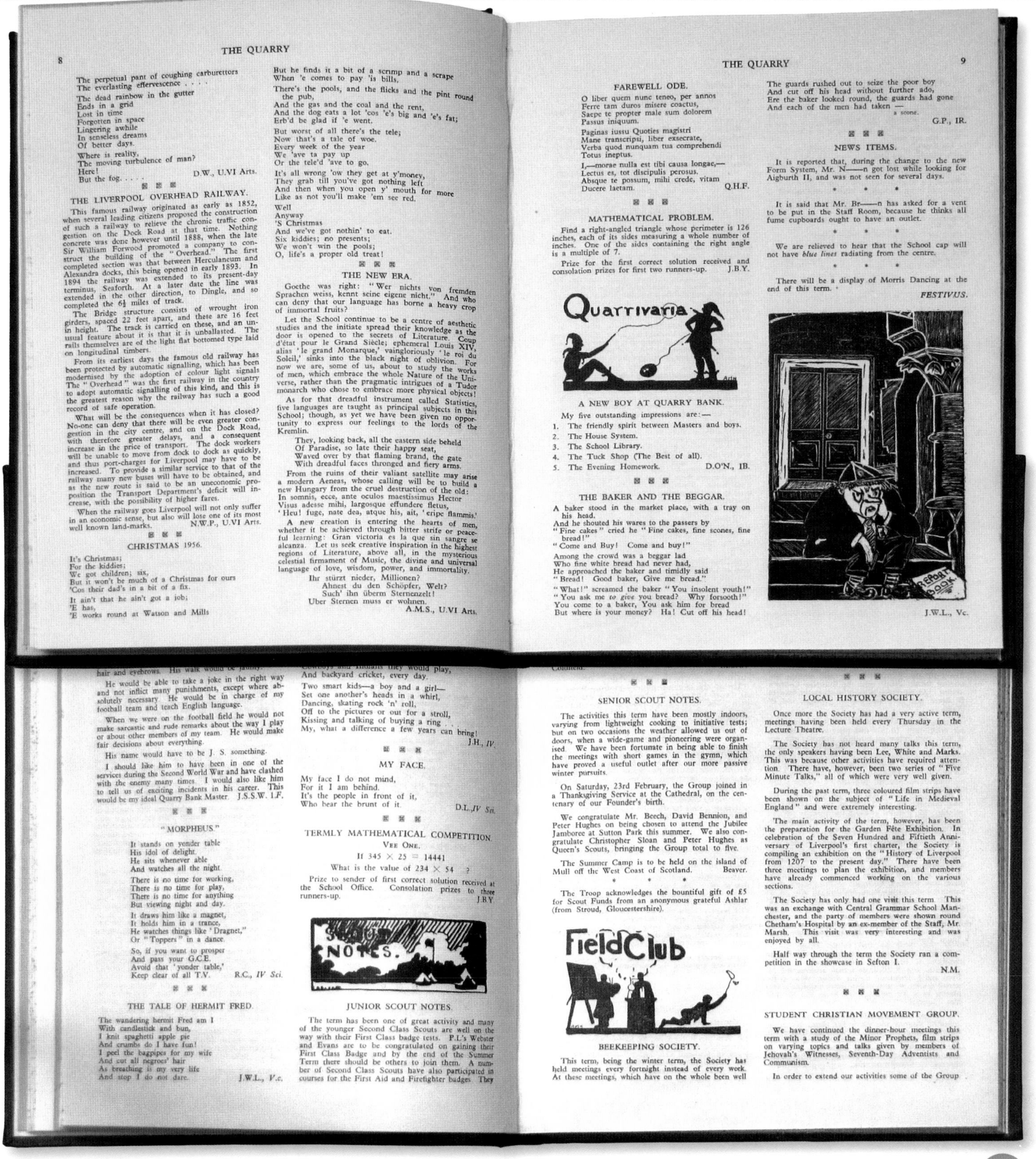

8 THE QUARRY

The perpetual pant of coughing carburettors
The everlasting effervescence . . . .
The dead rainbow in the gutter
Ends in a grid
Lost in time
Forgotten in space
Lingering awhile
In senseless dreams
Of better days.
Where is reality,
The moving turbulence of man?
Here!
But the fog. . . . . D.W., U.VI Arts.

THE LIVERPOOL OVERHEAD RAILWAY.

This famous railway originated as early as 1852, when several leading citizens proposed the construction of such a railway to relieve the chronic traffic congestion on the Dock Road at that time. Nothing concrete was done however until 1888, when the late Sir William Forwood promoted a company to construct the building of the "Overhead." The first completed section was that between Herculaneum and Alexandra docks, this being opened in early 1893. In 1894 the railway was extended to its present-day terminus, Seaforth. At a later date the line was extended in the other direction, to Dingle, and so completed the 6½ miles of track.

The Bridge structure consists of wrought iron girders, spaced 22 feet apart, and these are 16 feet in height. The track is carried on these, and an unusual feature about it is that it is unballasted. The rails themselves are of the light flat bottomed type laid on longitudinal timbers.

From its earliest days the famous old railway has been protected by automatic signalling, which has been modernised by the adoption of colour light signals The "Overhead" was the first railway in the country to adopt automatic signalling of this kind, and this is the greatest reason why the railway has such a good record of safe operation.

What will be the consequences when it has closed? No-one can deny that there will be even greater congestion in the city centre, and on the Dock Road, with therefore greater delays, and a consequent increase in the price of transport. The dock workers will be unable to move from dock to dock as quickly, and thus port-charges for Liverpool may have to be increased. To provide a similar service to that of the railway many new buses will have to be obtained, and as the new route is said to be an uneconomic proposition the Transport Department's deficit will increase, with the possibility of higher fares.

When the railway goes Liverpool will not only suffer in an economic sense, but also will lose one of its most well known land-marks. N.W.P., U.VI Arts.

CHRISTMAS 1956.

It's Christmas;
For the kiddies;
We got children; six,
But it won't be much of a Christmas for ours
'Cos their dad's in a bit of a fix.
It ain't that he ain't got a job;
'E has,
'E works round at Watson and Mills
But he finds it a bit of a scrimp and a scrape
When 'e comes to pay 'is bills.
There's the pools, and the flicks and the pint round the pub,
And the gas and the coal and the rent,
And the dog eats a lot 'cos 'e's big and 'e's fat;
Erb'd be glad if 'e went.
But worst of all there's the tele;
Now that's a tale of woe.
Every week of the year
We 'ave ta pay up
Or the tele'd 'ave to go.
It's all wrong 'ow they get at y'money,
They grab till you've got nothing left
And then when you open y' mouth for more
Like as not you'll make 'em see red.
Well
Anyway
'S Christmas
And we've got nothin' to eat.
Six kiddies; no presents;
We won't win the pools;
O, life's a proper old treat!

THE NEW ERA.

Goethe was right: "Wer nichts von fremden Sprachen weiss, kennt seine eigene nicht." And who can deny that our language has borne a heavy crop of immortal fruits?

Let the School continue to be a centre of aesthetic studies and the initiate spread their knowledge as the door is opened to the secrets of Literature. Coup d'état pour le Grand Siècle; ephemeral Louis XIV, alias 'le grand Monarque,' vaingloriously 'le roi du Soleil,' sinks into the black night of oblivion. For now we are, some of us, about to study the works of men, which embrace the whole Nature of the Universe, rather than the pragmatic intrigues of a Tudor monarch who chose to embrace more physical objects!

As for that dreadful instrument called Statistics, five languages are taught as principal subjects in this School; though, as yet we have been given no opportunity to express our feelings to the lords of the Kremlin.

They, looking back, all the eastern side beheld
Of Paradise, so late their happy seat,
Waved over by that flaming brand, the gate
With dreadful faces thronged and fiery arms.

From the ruins of their valiant satellite may arise a modern Aeneas, whose calling will be to build a new Hungary from the cruel destruction of the old:
In somnis, ecce, ante oculos maestissimus Hector
Visus adesse mihi, largosque effundere fletus,
'Heu! fuge, nate dea, atque his, ait, 'eripe flammis.'

A new creation is entering the hearts of men, whether it be achieved through bitter strife or peaceful learning: Gran victoria es la que sin sangre se alcanza. Let us seek creative inspiration in the highest regions of Literature, above all, in the mysterious celestial firmament of Music, the divine and universal language of love, wisdom, power, and immortality.

Ihr stürzt nieder, Millionen?
Ahnest du den Schöpfer, Welt?
Such' ihn überm Sternenzelt!
Uber Sternen muss er wohnen.
A.M.S., U.VI Arts.

THE QUARRY 9

FAREWELL ODE.

O liber quem nunc teneo, per annos
Ferre tam duros misere coactus,
Saepe te propter male sum dolorem
Passus iniquum.
Paginas iussu Quoties magistri
Mane transcripsi, liber exsecrate,
Verba quod nunquam tua comprehendi
Totus ineptus.
I,—morae nulla est tibi causa longae,—
Lectus es, tot discipulis perosus.
Absque te possum, mihi crede, vitam
Ducere laetam. Q.H.F.

MATHEMATICAL PROBLEM.

Find a right-angled triangle whose perimeter is 126 inches, each of its sides measuring a whole number of inches. One of the sides containing the right angle is a multiple of 7.

Prize for the first correct solution received and consolation prizes for first two runners-up. J.B.Y.

Quarrivaria

A NEW BOY AT QUARRY BANK.

My five outstanding impressions are:—
1. The friendly spirit between Masters and boys.
2. The House System.
3. The School Library.
4. The Tuck Shop (The Best of all).
5. The Evening Homework. D.O'N., IB.

THE BAKER AND THE BEGGAR.

A baker stood in the market place, with a tray on his head.
And he shouted his wares to the passers by
"Fine cakes" cried he "Fine cakes, fine scones, fine bread!"
"Come and Buy! Come and buy!"
Among the crowd was a beggar lad
Who fine white bread had never had,
He approached the baker and timidly said
"Bread! Good baker, Give me bread."
"What!" screamed the baker "You insolent youth!"
"You ask me *to give* you bread? Why forsooth!"
You come to a baker, You ask him for bread
But where is your money? Ha! Cut off his head!
The guards rushed out to seize the poor boy
And cut off his head without further ado,
Ere the baker looked round, the guards had gone
And each of the men had taken —
a scone.
G.P., IR.

NEWS ITEMS.

It is reported that, during the change to the new Form System, Mr. N——n got lost while looking for Aigburth II, and was not seen for several days.

* * *

It is said that Mr. Br——n has asked for a vent to be put in the Staff Room, because he thinks all fume cupboards ought to have an outlet.

* * *

We are relieved to hear that the School cap will not have *blue lines* radiating from the centre.

* * *

There will be a display of Morris Dancing at the end of this term.

FESTIVUS.

REPORT BOOK

J.W.L., Vc.

hair and eyebrows. His walk would be jaunty.

He would be able to take a joke in the right way and not inflict many punishments, except where absolutely necessary. He would be in charge of my football team and teach English language.

When we were on the football field he would not make sarcastic and rude remarks about the way I play or about other members of my team. He would make fair decisions about everything.

His name would have to be J. S. something.

I should like him to have been in one of the services during the Second World War and have clashed with the enemy many times. I would also like him to tell us of exciting incidents in his career. This would be my ideal Quarry Bank Master. J.S.S.W. 1*F*.

"MORPHEUS."

It stands on yonder table
His idol of delight.
He sits whenever able
And watches all the night.
There is no time for working,
There is no time for play,
There is no time for anything
But viewing night and day.
It draws him like a magnet,
It holds him in a trance,
He watches things like 'Dragnet,"
Or "Toppers" in a dance.
So, if you want to prosper
And pass your G.C.E.
Avoid that 'yonder table,'
Keep clear of all T.V. R.C., *IV Sci.*

THE TALE OF HERMIT FRED.

The wandering hermit Fred am I
With candlestick and bun,
I knit spaghetti apple pie
And crumbs do I have fun!
I peel the bagpipes for my wife
And cut all negroes' hair
As breathing is my very life
And stop I do not dare. J.W.L., *V.c.*

And backyard cricket, every day.
Two smart kids—a boy and a girl—
Set one another's heads in a whirl,
Dancing, skating rock 'n' roll,
Off to the pictures or out for a stroll,
Kissing and talking of buying a ring . . .
My, what a difference a few years can bring!
J.H., *IV.*

MY FACE.

My face I do not mind,
For it I am behind.
It's the people in front of it,
Who bear the brunt of it. D.L.,*IV Sci.*

TERMLY MATHEMATICAL COMPETITION.

VEE ONE.

If 345 × 25 = 14441

What is the value of 234 × 54 ?

Prize to sender of first correct solution received at the School Office. Consolation prizes to three runners-up. J.B.Y.

NOTES.

JUNIOR SCOUT NOTES.

The term has been one of great activity and many of the younger Second Class Scouts are well on the way with their First Class badge tests. P.L.'s Webster and Evans are to be congratulated on gaining their First Class Badge and by the end of the Summer Term there should be others to join them. A number of Second Class Scouts have also participated in courses for the First Aid and Firefighter badges. They

SENIOR SCOUT NOTES.

The activities this term have been mostly indoors, varying from lightweight cooking to initiative tests; but on two occasions the weather allowed us out of doors, when a wide-game and pioneering were organised. We have been fortunate in being able to finish the meetings with short games in the gymn, which have proved a useful outlet after our more passive winter pursuits.

On Saturday, 23rd February, the Group joined in a Thanksgiving Service at the Cathedral, on the centenary of our Founder's birth.

We congratulate Mr. Beech, David Bennion, and Peter Hughes on being chosen to attend the Jubilee Jamboree at Sutton Park this summer. We also congratulate Christopher Sloan and Peter Hughes as Queen's Scouts, bringing the Group total to five.

The Summer Camp is to be held on the island of Mull off the West Coast of Scotland. Beaver.

* * *

The Troop acknowledges the bountiful gift of £5 for Scout Funds from an anonymous grateful Ashlar (from Stroud, Gloucestershire).

FieldClub

BEEKEEPING SOCIETY.

This term, being the winter term, the Society has held meetings every fortnight instead of every week. At these meetings, which have on the whole been well

LOCAL HISTORY SOCIETY.

Once more the Society has had a very active term, meetings having been held every Thursday in the Lecture Theatre.

The Society has not heard many talks this term, the only speakers having been Lee, White and Marks. This was because other activities have required attention. There have, however, been two series of "Five Minute Talks," all of which were very well given.

During the past term, three coloured film strips have been shown on the subject of "Life in Medieval England" and were extremely interesting.

The main activity of the term, however, has been the preparation for the Garden Fête Exhibition. In celebration of the Seven Hundred and Fiftieth Anniversary of Liverpool's first charter, the Society is compiling an exhibition on the "History of Liverpool from 1207 to the present day." There have been three meetings to plan the exhibition, and members have already commenced working on the various sections.

The Society has only had one visit this term. This was an exchange with Central Grammar School Manchester, and the party of members were shown round Chetham's Hospital by an ex-member of the Staff, Mr. Marsh. This visit was very interesting and was enjoyed by all.

Half way through the term the Society ran a competition in the showcase in Sefton I.
N.M.

STUDENT CHRISTIAN MOVEMENT GROUP.

We have continued the dinner-hour meetings this term with a study of the Minor Prophets, film strips on varying topics and talks given by members of Jehovah's Witnesses, Seventh-Day Adventists and Communism.

In order to extend our activities some of the Group

day write a song about his Uncle Albert (which became number one in the United States) as well as brother Mike and their Auntie Gin and Uncle Ian in "Let 'Em In."

Paul became a Boy Scout and enjoyed outdoor pursuits, but his passion lay in music. In 1956 his parents bought him a trumpet for his birthday, but he traded it for a guitar, the key instrument of the new rock 'n' roll music. Later that year, Mary McCartney died from breast cancer, and Jim, Paul, and Mike were devastated. Psychologists might see a link between this loss and Paul's first-known composition, "I've Lost My Little Girl." "I remember Paul playing 'I've Lost My Little Girl' in his bedroom at Forthlin Road," says school friend Ian James. "I was very impressed; I had never thought of writing a song myself."

Paul and Ian attended the Liverpool Institute (the Inny). Prior to the 1950s, its most famous student was the comedian Arthur Askey, but by the late 1950s the students included many who would go on to illustrious careers: Paul and Mike McCartney, George Harrison, Neil Aspinall (the Beatles' road manager), Len Garry (Quarrymen), John Duff Lowe (Quarrymen), Les Chadwick (Gerry and the Pacemakers), Stu Slater (Mojos), and Don Andrew and Colin Manley (Remo Four), as well as Peter Sissons (BBC-TV newsreader), Steven Norris (a British politician), and Derek Hatton (a controversial local politician). One pupil, Bill Kenwright, went on to be a recording artist, an actor in the TV soap *Coronation Street*, a West End impresario, and the chairman of Everton Football Club.

It was at the Liverpool Institute that friendships developed based on a mutual love of music: listening to record collections, discussing the latest releases, and practicing at school and at each other's houses. Not surprisingly, other members of Paul's and George's peer group would go on to join bands that would also contribute to the genesis of Liverpool's Merseybeat music scene.

Opposite, top left: Paul McCartney's childhood home, Forthlin Road, Allerton.
Opposite, top right: Paul and younger brother Mike on a family holiday in North Wales.
Opposite: Paul (above) and Ian James (below) in "Inny" school uniform.
Above: Paul, his dad, Jim, and Mike in the back garden at Forthlin Road.
Top, right: John Duff Lowe, member of the Quarrymen.
Right: Neil Aspinall, future Beatles road manager and MD of Apple Corps.

"Paul and I would visit each other's houses and listen to records and play guitars," recalls Ian James. "My collection was mainly Fats Domino, Jerry Lee Lewis, Chuck Berry, Carl Perkins, and Elvis Presley. I enjoyed going round to Forthlin Road—Paul would play the piano, I would play guitar, and Mike would be on drums. We would make a heck of a racket in the front room, and Paul's dad would be trying to place bets on the telephone in the other room. He would come in and complain, and we would have to be quiet for a few minutes. Jim McCartney was quite a character, and I used to have a great time there."

After school the two boys would visit the record shops—NEMS, Currys, and Cranes—to hear the latest releases in the listening booths. They would seek out the traveling

fairs at Sefton Park and Speke. "We would stand around the waltzer [a carnival ride akin to a more staid Tilt-A-Whirl] as they would be playing the latest rock 'n' roll hits," explains Ian. "The first time I heard 'Heartbreak Hotel' was at the fairground at Southport—I was transfixed."

Ian came from a musical family: his grandfather was the bandmaster at Dingle Salvation Army, and he had seven brothers who all played musical instruments—guitars, zithers, cornets, and banjos. When skiffle and rock 'n' roll exploded on the music scene, it created excitement among the teenagers, so Ian's grandparents bought him a guitar from the Liverpool music store Hessy's, and it was on this very guitar that Ian taught Paul his first chords. "I do remember teaching Paul the chords to 'Twenty Flight Rock.' I was playing right-handed. I might have changed the strings around for Paul, but that would have been quite a lengthy process, so it's more likely that he learned it right-handed."

Above: The Liverpool Institute is now home to the Liverpool Institute for Performing Arts (LIPA) that was founded by Paul and opened in 1996.

Opposite, clockwise: Top: Liverpool Institute Speech Day program, December 1959. Paul won a special prize for art. Below: The "Inny's" school play production of *Saint Joan*, by George Bernard Shaw. Paul played the part of an assessor. Bill Kenwright, impresario and fellow pupil at the "Inny," has called Paul a "born actor."

THE CITY OF LIVERPOOL

LIVERPOOL INSTITUTE HIGH SCHOOL

SPEECH DAY

TUESDAY, DECEMBER 15th, 1959

The PRIZES will be Distributed
and the ADDRESS given by

THE RIGHT HONO

THE VISCOUNT

PRIZE LIST, 1959

FORM PRIZES

	Prizewinner
	P. K. Cripps
	A. R. Prince
	W. Reade
	R. J. Butcher
	D. A. Lunt
	S. G. Saunders
	P. Cartmel
	W. G. Jones
	C. N. Prince
	R. T. Brown
	R. Lewis
	G. J. Breden
	D. H. Slater
	M. A. Hill
	J. D. Chambers
	T. J. Kenwright
	J. Hess
	F. Phillips
	C. Morgan
	R. Bivon
	R. Y. Sharp
	L. Hand
	Morton
	Jones
	Jones
	Evans

FOUNDATION PRIZES

The Lord Derby Prizes :
Mathematics ... ... D. J. Whittake
Chemistry ... ... A. M. Zalin
French ... ... M. F. McNaughte
German ... ... J. R. P. McKenzie

William Durning Holt Prizes :
English Essay ... ... J. D. Lunt
Latin ... ... R. T. Crofts
Physics ... ... J. R. Conder

Samuel Booth Prizes :
English Literature ... ... D. Reed
Greek ... ... R. T. Crofts

F. S. Milliken Prize for History ... ... L. Bivon

Arthur Damsell Prizes for Arithmetic : Senior ... ... A. J. Cowan
Junior ... ... D. H. Mawdsley

Sir Frederick Radcliffe Prizes for Elocution : Senior ... ... R. S. Pybus
Junior ... ... B. R. West

George Herbert Allen Prize for British Commonwealth History ... D. S. Rudnick

Agnes Lunt Prize for Lower Sixths ... ... G. I. Davies

Kenneth Boswell Prize for Public Service ... ... J. M. Radcliffe

Sir Donald MacAlister Prize for Public Service ... { R. T. Crofts
{ W. J. Rigby

SPECIAL PRIZES

Prize for Music ... ... D. Norris
Prize for Spanish ... ... J. D. Lunt
Prize for Latin and Greek Verses—given by Mr. Bentliff ... R. T. Crofts
Prize for Art ... ... J. P. McCartney
Prize for French—given by the French Consul ... F. J. McKie

SAINT JO

ROBERT DE BAUL
STEWARD
JOAN
BERTRAND DE POU
ARCHBISHOP OF R
MGR. DE LA TRÉMO
COURT PAGE
GILLES DE RAIS
CAPTAIN LA HIRE
THE DAUPHIN (later Charles VII)
DUCHESS DE LA TRÉMOUILLE
DUNOIS, BASTARD OF ORLEANS
DUNOIS' PAGE
RICHARD DE BEAUCHAMP, EARL OF WARWICK
CHAPLAIN DE STOGUMBER
WARWICK'S PAGE
PETER CAUCHON, BISHOP OF BEAUVAIS
THE INQUISITOR
DE COURCELLES
D'ESTIVET
BROTHER MARTIN LADVENU
EXECUTIONER

DAVID WRIGHT
RAYMOND IRLAM
LACHLAN MACRAE
RODNEY OTHEN
STEPHEN HARLOW
GRAHAME SETTLE
JOHN CUTHELL
BRIAN WILSON
ALAN BREEZE
JEFFERY MORGAN
BRIAN WEST
MALCOLM BROWN
RAYMOND PHILLIPS
PETER SISSONS
PATRICK RADCLIFFE
STEVEN NORRIS
HOWARD PAUL
ANTHONY ZALIN
DAVID WILLIAMS
IAN ROBERTSON
PHILIP JELF
DAVID JONES

ASSESSORS : BRIAN PARKINSON, IAIN TAYLOR, JAMES WOODS, PAUL McCARTNEY, DAVID MOORE, LESLIE TROW, ALAN JONES, PAUL NENER, ANDREW WALLARD, GEOFFREY LATHAM, ROBERT NELSON.

COURTIERS : MICHAEL PEARSON, ANTHONY ARCHER, JOHN MACLEAN, TERENCE QUINN, NORMAN BROOKS, GEORGE MEADOWS, KENNETH MARTIN, DAVID KELLY, PAUL WINCKLES, LEONARD RAWLINSON, JOSEPH CAPEK.

SOLDIERS : PETER MARKS, PAUL ELLISON, REGINALD BLYTH, DAVID NORRIS.

THE PLAY PRODUCED BY MR. ALAN DURBAND

SCENE 1: THE CASTLE AT VAUCOULEURS

SCENE 2: ANTECHAMBER AND THRONE ROOM AT CHINON

INTERVAL OF TEN MINUTES
Patrons are asked to remain seated.

SCENE 3: THE BANKS OF THE RIVER LOIRE, NEAR ORLEANS

SCENE 4: THE EARL OF WARWICK'S TENT IN THE ENGLISH CAMP

INTERVAL OF TWENTY MINUTES
Refreshments will be served in the canteen.
Patrons are requested to return promptly to their seats when the bell rings.

SCENE 5: THE AMBULATORY OF RHEIMS CATHEDRAL

SCENE 6: A HALL IN THE CASTLE AT ROUEN

The action of the play takes place between February 1429 and May 1431.

Paul, having passed his eleven-plus exams, was a year ahead of George Harrison. It was a proud moment for George's parents when he entered the Liverpool Institute as a student in 1954. "Our dad wanted us to have the best education possible," says George's sister, Louise. "After that, he thought we should all have training or apprenticeships." Not, it's worth noting, universities, which were then the province of the brighter, more scholarly pupils.

Fellow pupil Don Andrew, later with the Remo Four, recalls Paul and George playing their guitars in the school's music room. "We were allowed to bring our guitars in on the last day of term, and I remember seeing George, Paul, and Len Garry doing Carl Perkins and Elvis Presley numbers. George was everybody's idol because he had an electric guitar in a big black case—the rest of us had Spanish guitars in polythene bags."

"I would often discuss guitars with George, as we would be on the same bus in the morning," remembers fellow pupil Les Chadwick, who later became a member of Gerry and the Pacemakers. "He was an avid Chet Atkins fan, and he had an uncle who sent him some albums from the States. We would try and copy anything that we thought was good."

"We wanted to do a perfect imitation when we heard those old records, and Paul was a very good mimic," comments Ian James. "Usually before morning assembly, there would be a crowd around him and he would be reviewing the previous night's radio programs like *The Goon Show*. He could do all the silly voices very well. He could also sing Little Richard songs perfectly."

The Goon Show was a popular radio comedy show broadcast from 1951–60 on the otherwise staid BBC Home Service. It was different from any comedy that had gone before. Spike Milligan used the show to mock the ridiculous discipline he had witnessed while serving in the forces, but the Liverpool lads saw that the same style of mimicry could be used to lampoon schoolteachers and parents. The fact that authority figures had little time for rock 'n' roll music and freakish comedy secured the popularity of both among the young.

Paul McCartney was bright and would have been expected to pass seven or eight O-levels in the same examination year, but like John and George his mind was elsewhere. He passed one O-level in 1957 and four more in 1958. He was good at languages, passing in German, French, and Spanish, and he had the potential to go to university. When Paul first went to Hamburg with the Beatles, he wrote sardonically to the headmaster, "I've got a great job in Germany and I'm earning £15 a week." In 1997, an old math book of Paul's, which was filled with scribbling and drawings, fetched £23,000 at auction.

Opposite, top: George Harrison in the living room at Upton Green in 1956. He's playing his first guitar, an acoustic Dutch instrument bought by his father for under £3.

Opposite, below: George's early childhood home in Arnold Grove. When he was six, the family moved to Upton Green, on the Speke Council Estate—just a few streets away from Paul in Forthlin Road.

Above: Great Charlotte Street in the center of Liverpool, 1959. To the left of the picture is Blackler's department store where George was apprenticed as an electrician. A branch of NEMS was on the other side of the road.

George Harrison, born on February 25, 1943, was the last of four children of Harold and Louise Harrison. George was born at home in 12 Arnold Grove, a small terraced house with an outside toilet, in a cul-de-sac in Wavertree. In 1950, the family was offered a council house (a British form of public housing), so they moved to 25 Upton Green, Speke.

"There were six of us in the family, and we had a lot of fun together," comments Louise Harrison. "Mum and Dad were very exuberant and lively. Dad was a bus driver, and that encouraged George's interest in driving and, later on, racing cars. They were funny and witty too, and they always look happy in the old photographs. They did exercise some discipline, and they encouraged us to have good self-esteem, which held us all in good stead. As soon as George heard Elvis, he wanted to be a musician, but there was nothing unusual in that. Thousands of young boys felt the same way."

George's scholastic record at the Liverpool Institute was unimpressive, and in 1959 he was told to repeat his O-level year. This held no appeal for him, so he enrolled as a trainee electrician in Blackler's department store in the city center. His brothers, Harry and Peter, were working as a car mechanic and welder, and his father thought he might leave his job as a bus driver and set up a family garage business. George, however, had little interest in wiring the Christmas lights for Blackler's grotto; for him, learning to be an electrician meant he could repair his own amplifiers.

John, Paul, and George had received a good education, one of the best in Liverpool, although at the time their families thought the boys had squandered their opportunities. However, life for the young Ringo Starr, born Richard Starkey, was very different.

Ringo's father, also named Richard, was a Liverpool docker who later became a baker. He had married Elsie Gleave in 1936, and their son was born at home at 9 Madryn Street in the Dingle, three miles south of the city center, on July 7, 1940. When the couple divorced in 1943, Elsie moved to

Opposite far left: Ringo and his quiff in 1958.

Opposite: Admiral Grove, Liverpool 8, in 1971. Ringo lived here until The Fabs moved to London. The street was featured in Don Howarth's BBC documentary, made as Beatlemania hit in 1963. Ringo is mobbed as he steps out of the front door and makes his way into the open-top sports car being driven by George. The Empress pub featured on the cover of Ringo's *Liverpool 8* album is just to the left of shot.

Right: Contemporaries of the Beatles in the late 1950s and early '60s, Rory Storm and the Hurricanes were one of the most popular acts on the Liverpool and Hamburg club scenes. Ringo Starr was the drummer for the Hurricanes before joining the Beatles in August 1962.

a smaller home in an adjacent street, Admiral Grove. She married Harry Graves, a painter and decorator for Liverpool Corporation, in 1953. Richie got on fine with his stepfather (whom he called his "stepladder"), and Harry bought him a drum kit. With his large nose, Richie thought he would never be a celebrity, but he joked that any insults went "in one nostril and out the other."

Richie went to St. Silas Church of England Primary School, like Ronnie Wycherley (later Billy Fury), but both of them had a considerable amount of time off sick. Richie's childhood medical history includes a burst appendix, pleurisy, and two months in a coma; persistent digestive problems gave him an equally poor attendance record at Dingle Vale Secondary Modern School. It's hardly surprising that his education suffered. He left school without taking O-levels, and Harry secured him a job, making playground climbing frames (better known in the United States as jungle gyms or monkey bars) at Henry Hunt & Son in Speke. He worked there for four

years, becoming a senior apprentice. Throughout this time, Ringo played drums in several high-quality local bands. He dreamed of settling in America, even writing to the Chamber of Commerce in Houston about possible employment. He loved the blues of Lightnin' Hopkins, who was based in Houston, and he became an American country music enthusiast, with some of his favorite songs finding their way into the Beatles' repertoire.

In May 1960 he left, according to his employment card, "to join a dance band at a Butlins camp for the season." That dance band was the Liverpool rock 'n' roll outfit Rory Storm and the Hurricanes. Ringo had previously played with the group; they were semi-pro so, along with the other members, he left his day job and went professional. It was while Ringo was playing with Rory Storm and the Hurricanes in Skegness on the Lincolnshire coast in the East of England that he got the offer to join the Beatles.

SCHOOL DAYS

Throughout their childhood and teenage years, the Beatles' musical influences, while listening to records at friends' houses or on the radio, were primarily American. They all shared a love of American rock 'n' roll—in particular, Elvis Presley, "the King," whose vibrant music leapt from the turntables, at least until he was conscripted in 1958, and outlandish performers such as Little Richard and Gene Vincent. The boys also had a love of surrealist humor inspired by the authority-mocking BBC comedy program *The Goon Show*. Two of the Goons' comedy team, Spike Milligan and Peter Sellers, recorded for George Martin at Parlophone, and the Goons' television performances were often directed by Richard Lester. Both Martin and Lester were to play important roles in the Beatles' creative life.

"I told John that I had a record by a guy who was, in my opinion, better than Elvis Presley. That got his attention, as he was a really keen Elvis fan. When I played the record to him and Pete, John was speechless. It was a memorable event, as John was never usually stuck for words. That record was 'Long Tall Sally' by Little Richard. I had bought the record on a school exchange program in Amsterdam. In the mid-'60s John Lennon was interviewed about what caused him to take up music, and, incredibly, he described this particular event at my house."

MICHAEL HILL, JOHN'S SCHOOL FRIEND AT QUARRY BANK

"We used to bring our guitars in on the last day of term when there weren't any lessons or when the examinations were over. I was into the British guitarist Bert Weedon and how he was playing his guitar, but Paul and George dismissed him in favor of American musicians. Paul could sing like Little Richard, and I was flabbergasted when I heard him sing. I can remember George coming in with his electric guitar, and I was going, 'Wow, how loud is that!'"

COLIN MANLEY (right) OF THE REMO FOUR, FELLOW PUPIL AT THE LIVERPOOL INSTITUTE

"Paul had a white sports jacket with black flecks in it, and I had a pale blue version. We would always wear them at the fairgrounds, as we thought that they were really cool. We also wore narrow trousers, as it was the trend at the time, and I took Paul to a tailor that I knew on Mill Street, and he would take in the width of the leg bottoms to whatever you wanted, so we went at lunchtime or after school. Paul's dad said to him once, 'Where did you get those trousers from?' and Paul replied, quite truthfully, 'They are the same trousers that I went out in this morning.'"

IAN JAMES, PAUL'S SCHOOL FRIEND AT THE LIVERPOOL INSTITUTE

"I'd known John Lennon since he was seven years old, and he never changed. The fame, the money, and the status he achieved never affected the fundamental person that he was. A lot of people become aware of their own self-importance, but that never happened to John, maybe because he was self-important from the time when I first met him. People were attracted to him because of his great confidence and terrific humor. He was very quick, and you didn't argue with him, as you were on a loser before you started."

PETE SHOTTON, JOHN LENNON'S BEST FRIEND

"George Harrison hardly ever had a school badge on. His mother hadn't sewn it on, and he would hold it in place with a paperclip and a pen and take it off immediately he got out of school. That is in keeping with his character—an air of rebellion."

RAY O'BRIEN, FELLOW PUPIL AT THE LIVERPOOL INSTITUTE

"We were sent to Bioletti's in Penny Lane for a haircut. Mr. Bioletti had this rule that if an adult entered the boys would have to wait. They would pinch our ears with the cutters and give us short back and sides. Mr. Bioletti's hands used to shake as he cut your hair. John joked that old man Bioletti cut through somebody's scalp once and you could see the brain moving, and that the barber got some sticking plaster and stuck the scalp back. John had a great imagination and was great fun as long as you were on his side."

DAVID ASHTON, SCHOOL FRIEND OF JOHN LENNON

ROCK 'N' ROLL

DURING THE BEATLES' CHILDHOODS, the British and American record charts consisted predominantly of love songs, religious ballads, and novelty numbers. Al Martino, Frank Sinatra, and Doris Day sang well, but they didn't excite young teenagers. The first sign of change came with Johnnie Ray. Always formally dressed, the "Prince of Wails" had an emotional intensity that hadn't been heard before. His 1954 single "Such a Night" not only topped the UK chart but was also banned by the BBC for sexual explicitness. In the same year, a former country and western group, Bill Haley and His Comets, made the Top 10 with a good-natured interpretation of Big Joe Turner's U.S. rhythm and blues hit "Shake, Rattle and Roll." A year later Bill was at number one with "Rock Around the Clock," the defining anthem of rock 'n' roll. Despite his kiss curl (surely the world's most ridiculous fashion), Haley looked like a Scout leader, and although he heralded in the new music, he was married, with a young family. His diaries reveal that he was more concerned about his hemorrhoids than with being a sex symbol. That role fell to Elvis Presley.

Presley grew up hearing black gospel and rhythm 'n' blues music, which had a marked effect on his style. The soon-to-be Beatles would not have been exposed to this style of music through listening to the safe popular music played on the BBC; instead, they were fired by the music of friends' record collections, or songs played at local funfairs. Paul McCartney, who released an album of standards in 2012, says, "My main roots are in the sing-along stuff like 'When the Red, Red, Robin Comes Bob-bob-bobbin' Along' and 'Carolina Moon.' I didn't know the origins of songs like 'Milkcow Blues Boogie' and 'That's All Right (Mama).' It's only later that I found out about Leadbelly, Arthur 'Big Boy' Crudup, and all the black guys."

Elvis had been recording for the Sun label in Memphis since 1954, but those records were not released in the UK at the

Above: Elvis Presley in a still from *Jailhouse Rock* (1958). Note George's hero, Scotty Moore, on guitar and D.J. Fontana on drums.

Opposite: A former prisoner, Huddie Ledbetter, known as Leadbelly, became a hugely influential folk singer, best known for "Rock Island Line" and "Goodnight Irene."

Right: Rhythm and blues singer Arthur "Big Boy" Crudup recorded "That's All Right (Mama)" and "My Baby Left Me," in 1946. Elvis recorded "That's All Right (Mama)" as his first single for Sun Records in 1954.

time. There is no evidence of any enterprising Cunard Yank bringing Elvis's records to Liverpool. Indeed, Elvis was not even heard nationally in the United States until he signed with RCA and released "Heartbreak Hotel" early in 1956. His sexual gyrations on *The Ed Sullivan Show* and other nationwide programs were not shown in the UK, but British teenagers were fascinated to read of the controversy, loved the music, and bought his records. From May to December 1956, Elvis made the UK

Left: Every songwriter wanted to write songs with the directness, simplicity, and melodic quality of Buddy Holly's. Paul McCartney would eventually purchase Buddy Holly's back catalog.
Opposite, left: Although in his thirties, Chuck Berry wrote about teenage life in America. Versions of two Chuck Berry classics were early recordings of both the Beatles and the Stones. The Beatles recorded "Roll Over Beethoven" on their second album, while the Rolling Stones' first hit single was "Come On."
Opposite, right: The king of skiffle, Lonnie Donegan, recording at Pye Records in the 1950s. Donegan's last week in the UK charts with Leadbelly's "Pick a Bale of Cotton" in 1962 coincided with the Beatles' debut single "Love Me Do."

Top 10 with "Heartbreak Hotel," "Blue Suede Shoes," "Hound Dog," and a lethargic "Blue Moon"—a performance that was arguably thirty years ahead of its time. Once Elvis had opened the musical doors, Little Richard, Gene Vincent, and Chuck Berry came marching through.

The impact of American rock 'n' roll music on the UK's youth culture also benefited from good timing. Before the 1950s, there was no such term as "teenage," as adolescents were supposed to behave like young adults. Sixteen-year-olds would want to look like their parents, whereas today the situation has been reversed. In the mid '50s the first teenage fashions were seen in the UK when males dressed in long velvet-collared jackets, drainpipe trousers, and sideburns.

As this outfit parodied an Edwardian style, they were called Teddy Boys. Many of them led the rock 'n' roll riots that accompanied stage shows and screenings of the films *The Blackboard Jungle* (1955) and *Rock Around the Clock* (1956). In Liverpool, Teddy Boys would tear up the cinema seats, and the police turned hoses on one excitable cinema crowd that insisted on dancing in the street after watching *Rock Around the Clock*.

Music historian Jon Savage comments, "You will find very few teenage songs before 1955. Frank Sinatra may have been the idol of the bobby-soxers, but he didn't sing about the joys of being seventeen. It wasn't until rock 'n' roll came along that people started writing self-consciously about teenage

life. Then came great songs like Chuck Berry's 'Sweet Little Sixteen,' Eddie Cochran's 'Summertime Blues,' and Dion and the Belmonts' 'A Teenager in Love.' The first record that the Shadows made as the Five Chesternuts was called 'Teenage Love,' and Lennon and McCartney's 'I Saw Her Standing There' was originally called 'Seventeen.'"

As rock 'n' roll exploded in America, something unexpected happened in the UK. Many British teens, especially university students, preferred jazz to pop music. Chris Barber's Jazz Band, for example, was a touring attraction. Lonnie Donegan had joined Barber's band as a banjo player, and Barber realized his potential as an idiosyncratic singer of American blues songs. He added skiffle sessions to their performances, featuring Donegan on vocals and guitar, himself on double

bass, and Beryl Bryden on washboard. In 1954, when the band recorded the album *New Orleans Joys* for Decca, they included Donegan's treatment of Leadbelly's "Rock Island Line," which was then released as a single and made the UK Top 10 in January 1956. Donegan went solo and recorded prolifically, singing of chain gangs, building dams, and escaping from the law. He heralded a skiffle craze—with the Vipers, Chas McDevitt, and Bob Cort having a short, limited success—and, more significantly, he encouraged youngsters to make music on cheap instruments. The UK was still recovering from the war, and forming a skiffle group for a youth club was conveniently inexpensive.

LIVERPOOL'S RECORDING ARTISTS

Opposite the Cavern on Mathew Street is the Liverpool Wall of Fame, where there is a disc for every number-one record from Liverpool: fifty-six of them, more than any other UK city outside of London. The Beatles are represented by seventeen discs and, with their songwriting abilities and solo records, twenty-seven UK number ones have a Beatle connection. Although the Beatles are responsible for almost half of the Liverpool number ones, the Wall demonstrates the considerable talent in Liverpool both before and after the Beatles.

Going way back, Liverpool has been a city of entertainment and has, as it were, punched above its weight. Comedian Ken Dodd points out the long line of Liverpool music hall performers; Ken is on the Wall himself, with "Tears," the biggest-selling record of 1965. "I know the rock 'n' rollers were slagging me off for coming out with this tuneful, sing-along song, but it didn't bother me. I knew I had the best song in the charts."

The UK record charts began in the *New Musical Express* in November 1952, and Liverpool had five number ones before the Beatles. Lita Roza, once a vocalist with Ted Heath and his orchestra, was the first British female to have a UK number one, albeit with a children's song that she didn't want to record: "How Much is that Doggie in the Window?" (1953). Singing late-night torch songs like "Man in a Raincoat" and "Love for Sale" was more to her liking. Lita Roza died in 2008, and her ashes were scattered on the Mersey.

The high-kicking and exuberant Frankie Vaughan topped the charts with "The Garden of Eden" (1957) and "Tower of Strength" (1961) and also climbed high with "The Green Door" and "There Must Be a Way." Although it was not a hit single, he is associated with the playful but romantic "Give Me the Moonlight." "The first time I tried out 'Give Me the Moonlight'

was at the Liverpool Empire," said Frankie, "and when I got to the part, 'If there's anyone in doubt, and they'd like to try me out,' someone shouted, ''Ere you are, Frankie, try me.' This was hilarious and led to me putting the giggle in the song. It's got that Liverpool sense of humor whenever I sing it."

Frankie often reflected on his upbringing in Liverpool's poverty-stricken Scotland Road, and he worked tirelessly for the National Association of Boys' Clubs. His 1957 film *These Dangerous Years* was set in the Dingle, but as he was nearly thirty, he was too old (and too square) to be playing a Teddy Boy.

Frankie discovered Mal Perry, who in 1958 made five singles for Fontana that sold well without making the charts. The former Quarry Bank schoolboy, who wrote his own single, "The Girl Next Door," had been writing songs since he was ten years old. Mal made an impression on John Lennon, as John was unaware of any others who were writing their own material at the time. When Brian Epstein arranged a signing at his NEMS record store for "Make Me a Miracle," he offered to manage him, but Mal informed him that he already had a manager—the splendidly named Woolfe Bednash.

The man who would be Bing, Michael Holliday, topped the charts with "The Story of My Life" (1958) and "Starry Eyed" (1960) and was Tex Tucker's voice in the puppet western *Four Feather Falls*. Holliday had a warm delivery, but he was very nervous, and he would write the lyrics to even his best-known songs on his cuffs. He died from an overdose in 1963.

Above: Frankie Vaughan and Marilyn Monroe in *Let's Make Love* (1960).
Opposite: Lita Roza became the first British female artist to have a number one when her single "How Much Is That Doggie in the Window?" reached the top spot in the UK charts, in 1953.
Top, from left: Michael Holliday seemed as relaxed as Perry Como but he was a bag of nerves; Billy Fury (left) was one of Larry Parnes's stable of stars. Brian Epstein modeled NEMS Enterprises on the Parnes Organisation; Larry Parnes renamed Chris Morris as Lance Fortune. Lance soon left Parnes and took the name with him, much to Parnes's annoyance. He wanted to use it for another artist, whom he then called Georgie Fame.

A significant omission from the Wall of Fame is Billy Fury, as most people would assume he had had number-one records. He was the UK's most convincing rock 'n' roll star; he started in Jack Good's ITV show, *Oh Boy!*, and had his first hit with "Maybe Tomorrow" in 1959. The following year he wrote and recorded *The Sound of Fury*, the only British album to replicate the sound from the Sun Studios in Memphis. The live album *We Want Billy!* demonstrates that screaming for Liverpool performers didn't start with the Beatles. Fury was reluctant to speak on stage, as he thought people would hear his accent and assume he was common. How wrong can you be?

Fury soared to major fame with romantic beat-ballads like "Halfway to Paradise" (1961), "Jealousy" (1961), and "Like I've Never Been Gone" (1963), and he had eleven Top 10 singles without making number one. His most iconic record, the highly sensual "Wondrous Place" (1960), was only a minor success, but now it is used to describe Liverpool itself. Billy Fury had a damaged heart from contracting rheumatic fever as a child, and he died while making a comeback in 1983.

In 1960, two more teenage heartthrobs from the area, Michael Cox and Lance Fortune, made the Top 10 with "Angela Jones" and "Be Mine," respectively. Although Johnny Gentle wrote and recorded several singles and was managed by leading promoter Larry Parnes, he never made the charts. Not only does he play a part in the Beatles' story, but he also performed on the last night of Eddie Cochran and Gene Vincent's tour in April 1960, just prior to Cochran's death.

2 "CUT OUT THE BLOODY ROCK 'N' ROLL!"

"A guitar's all right, John, but you'll never make a living out of it."
AUNT MIMI

Left: Before the fête at St. Peter's Church in Woolton on July 6, 1957, the participants paraded around the village on floats. Here are the Quarrymen getting ready to perform (left to right): Pete Shotton, Eric Griffiths, Len Garry (with his back to us), John Lennon, Colin Hanton, and Rodney Verso Davis (to give him his full name) in glasses. Note the Quarrymen sign. The photograph was taken by James Davis, Rod's father.

Sixteen-year-old John Lennon liked what he heard on the BBC on the rare occasions when the presenters deigned to play rock 'n' roll and skiffle. Postwar, the BBC wished to uphold the notion of prewar respectability, regulating the amount of American music that graced the airwaves. However, the commercial station Radio Luxembourg, which was broadcast from the Grand Duchy of Luxembourg—a tiny country bordered by Belgium, France, and Germany—had no such restrictions; therefore the sounds of Buddy Holly and Chuck Berry could be heard, when the poor reception allowed.

John's mother, Julia, showed him banjo chords, which he then transferred to the guitar that Aunt Mimi had bought him. According to John, Julia liked rock 'n' roll; if true, this was highly unusual. Hardly any forty-somethings enjoyed rock 'n' roll in the 1950s.

Surprisingly for someone so impatient, John wanted to learn the instrument, and he and his friend Eric Griffiths sought professional instruction. "We both went to a guitar teacher in Hunts Cross," explained Eric. "But we decided that it was boring, trying to learn to play properly and not being able to get a tune out of it. John's mother, Julia, played the banjo, so she retuned the guitar strings, and we both played in that manner until Paul McCartney joined the band. We were just using four strings, and the top two strings were tuned to the fourth. We were interested in playing rather than learning."

Around March 1957, John decided to form his own band, and he looked to his school friends. This resulted in three of them—John, Eric, and Rod Davis—playing banjo chords. Rod Davis remembers, "I had bought a banjo from my uncle, and if he'd sold me his guitar instead, I might have been decent enough to keep Paul McCartney out of the band. That was our big limitation. McCartney could play the guitar like a guitar, and we couldn't, and let's face it, a banjo doesn't look good in a rock group."

The weakest musical member in a skiffle group was usually given the washboard; in this case, it fell to Pete Shotton. "I had a lack of musical ability, apart from the fact that I can just about keep rhythm," says Pete, "and John told me to give it a go. I viewed the washboard as a joke rather than

Top: Nigel Walley (center) surrounded by Beth Shotton (Pete's wife), Cynthia Powell and her mother Lil, John Lennon, and Pete Shotton.
Above: Nigel Walley printed a run of business cards advertising himself as the manager of the Quarrymen.
Opposite: The Quarrymen at a street party in Rosebery Street, Toxteth, on June 22, 1957 to celebrate the 750th anniversary of King John giving Liverpool a royal charter, an indication that Liverpool people will celebrate anything. During the party, some local youths wanted to beat up Lennon, and he had to take cover.

as an instrument, but there wouldn't have been a band if I hadn't been in it. I didn't like performing; I was shy and embarrassed, as I knew I wasn't a musician."

The one-string tea-chest bass was also open to untried musicians, but the Quarrymen had difficulty in finding the right person. Nigel Walley didn't enjoy the role and instead had business cards printed to say he was the Quarrymen's manager. Ivan Vaughan, who had introduced John to Paul, had a brief trial; Bill Smith wouldn't turn up for rehearsals and then went to sea. Their fourth choice, Len Garry, joined them.

Now the group required a drummer. Colin Hanton did not attend Quarry Bank High, but he traveled to work on the same bus as Eric. "I used to listen to jazz records and play the beat on the furniture. My parents said that if I bought drums, I could play them in the house. I went to Frank Hessy's music store and bought a drum kit in installments of ten shillings a week. It was £34 in total. Eric asked if he could hear me play. I set up the drums, put on a record, and played along to it, and he said, 'Come and meet the lads.' That was it. I was a Quarryman."

As John and Pete were rebellious, it is curious that the band was named after their school. "I said the Quarrymen, without even thinking about it," explains Pete Shotton. "As well as Quarry Bank, we lived by the quarry in Woolton, and maybe there was a subconscious thought about the quarry being stone, and the stone being rock."

The Quarrymen began with skiffle songs like "Rock Island Line" and "Maggie May." The songs were easy to play and were very acceptable to audiences, but fairly soon the band progressed to playing the early, and more challenging, Elvis Presley tunes, such as "Blue Moon of Kentucky," "All Shook Up," and "I'm Left, You're Right, She's Gone."

Although it was not stated as such, the others took the Quarrymen to be John Lennon's group. As Rod Davis remarks, "Well, there was only one microphone, and he had it. Len could sing reasonably well, and I remember Eric and me having a go, but we didn't come up with much. We didn't have the voices to do it, but John did."

John Lennon had the voice, but he didn't always know the lyrics to the songs. "Unless you bought the record, you wouldn't know all the words," says Rod Davis. "When the record was played on the radio, you would shout for a pen and start scribbling down the verse, or you would go to a booth in a record shop and listen to it until you got thrown out. John would fill in the missing words, and that's how we got the bit about the penitentiary that is in 'Come Go with Me,' which scanned and fitted in with the themes of skiffle songs. I also remember him rewriting 'Streamline Train' as 'Long Black Train.'"

Like many of the early skiffle groups on Merseyside, the Quarrymen took part in talent contests at ballrooms and theaters. The organizers didn't pay the performers, so it was a cheap and popular way of arranging an evening's entertainment. Eric Griffiths recalled, "Perversely, the best gig was at a competition at the Locarno Ballroom. We played well, but the audience wanted skiffle, and we got booed for playing rock 'n' roll. But all the gigs were good. I can't think of anywhere we came away absolutely devastated."

On June 9, 1957, the Quarrymen played the Empire Theatre on Lime Street, the biggest venue in Liverpool, for *The Carroll Levis Discovery Show*—a '50s talent competition for youngsters. "The preliminary heat was on a Sunday, and my mother wouldn't let me

Above: The Grafton (top) and the Locarno (below—now the Olympia) were two ballrooms next to each other on West Derby Road. The Beatles played both venues, but the Grafton was seen as more old-fashioned, still promoting ballroom dancing in the '60s.

THE QUARRYMEN AND THE SKIFFLE CRAZE

By the late '50s, skiffle had captured the imagination of young teenagers across Britain. Household objects were used as instruments, which made the creation and performance of music accessible to all. Thousands of skiffle groups across England played in coffee bars, jazz clubs, and bars, as well as at the many talent competitions across the UK.

Above: Taken on the day of St. Peter's church fête, July 6, 1957, Quarryman Rod Davis with his younger brother Bernie clutching the washboard, and his sister Rosemary in her Brownie uniform ready to take part in the day's parade. Bernie is now a bluegrass musician, and proficient at playing the saw.

"Lonnie Donegan was the messiah. Before then, you had to have professional tuition, and you had to learn the chords. Lonnie comes along and says, 'You can all play music. Get a drum and bang on it, make a tea-chest bass and twang the string, get a washboard and some thimbles: it doesn't matter whether you're good or bad, just enjoy it.' Lonnie was taking the music from the professionals and giving it to the grass roots, although he was brilliant himself."

PETE SHOTTON

"I remember the Quarrymen coming round to our house to practice, and they used to shoo me away. Their guitars smelt strongly of Woodbine cigarettes, and they would practice for hours. I remember the couch they sat on; my mother regretted that she didn't cut it up and sell bits of it."

BERNIE DAVIS, Rod Davis's younger brother and a Merseyside bluegrass musician

"I vaguely remember some bloke in a dark jacket, but I don't remember him playing 'Twenty Flight Rock' at all. If Paul McCartney had played the guitar competently in front of me, I'm sure I would remember it, so maybe I went for a pee. The greatest moment in rock 'n' roll history and Rod Davis suffered from incontinence."

ROD DAVIS, THE QUARRYMEN, ON THE DAY OF THE FÊTE

THE DAY PAUL MET JOHN

GARDEN FETE

ST. PETER'S CHURCH FIELD

WOOLTON PARISH CHURCH   Rector: M.

Saturday, 6th July,

at 3 p.m.

ADMISSION BY PROGRAMME

CHILDREN 3d.

PROCEEDS IN AID OF CHURCH

STALLS —

ST. PETER'S CHURCH IN CHURCH ROAD, Woolton, is a fine example of Victorian Gothic architecture. It was built by wealthy merchants in 1887, and, being the parish church, it was well attended. Although its primary purpose was worship, tourists also visited, as they wanted to see the magnificent views from the bell tower.

In the 1950s, the church had annual garden fêtes, and on July 6, 1957, the Quarrymen were billed to appear in one, alongside the Band of the Cheshire Yeomanry, a police dog display, a fancy dress parade, and the crowning of the Rose Queen. The booking came through Pete Shotton's mother, who recommended them as ideal entertainment for the youngsters.

At 2 p.m., a procession of floats paraded through the local streets, with the Quarrymen on the back of a coal truck. Their first performance was on a makeshift stage in a large field in the church grounds; finally, at 8 p.m., they played alongside the George Edwards Band for the Grand Dance in the church hall.

It was a lovely summer afternoon, and the Quarrymen were well received, probably because most of the churchgoers had never seen a live rock 'n' roll or skiffle band before and were intrigued. Ivan Vaughan wanted to

PROGRAMME

IDESHOWS — ICE CREAM — LEMONADE

and Refreshments in large Marquee situated behind the hut.

ch Road, via Allerton cross Avenue; returning	3-30 p.m. to 5-00 p.m.	MUSICAL SELECTIONS by the Band of the Cheshire (Earl of Chester) Yeomanry. Band- master: H. Abraham. (By permission of Lt.-Col. G. C. V. Churton, M.C., M.B.E.).
heshire Yeomanry. uth Club during the		
OSE QUEEN (Miss wall JONES.	4-15 p.m.	THE QUARRY MEN SKIFFLE GROUP.
	5-15 p.m.	DISPLAY by the City of Liverpool Police Dogs. By kind permission of the Chief Constable and Watch Committee.
Fuller at the Church	5-45 p.m.	THE QUARRY MEN SKIFFLE GROUP

GRAND DANCE in the CHURCH HALL

VARDS BAND also The Quarry Men Skiffle Group

TICKETS 2/-

REFRESHMENTS AT MODERATE PRICES.

Far left: The Quarrymen on Saturday, July 6, 1957.
Center insets: The famous Garden Fête program. Three gigs in a day—the Quarrymen were obviously preparing for Hamburg!
Below: Modern views of St. Peter's Church Woolton and the gravestone of Eleanor Rigby.

says Len Garry. "He even put it behind his back to play it." (Paul was not only showing off, he was predating Jimi Hendrix by several years.)

Paul was in the church hall for only twenty minutes, but that was long enough for John to determine he should be a Quarryman. His only reservation was the realization that Paul had enough talent to challenge his leadership.

About ten days after the fête, Pete Shotton met Paul as he was riding through Woolton. "He got off his bike and I said, 'Oh, by the way, do you want to join the group?' He thought about it for a moment and then said, 'Okay.' He then got on his bike and buggered off."

"I only met Paul on one occasion after the Woolton fête," says Rod Davis, "and it was at Aunt Mimi's a fortnight later. He dropped in to hear us practicing. From my point of view, I was the person he was replacing—it's like Pete Best—you're the guy who doesn't know what's going on."

The garden fête was revived in 1997 with the intention of recreating the day John met Paul. The Quarrymen played, albeit without their most famous members, and unveiled a plaque on the church hall. As Rod Davis remarked, "I hope we didn't sound any worse than we did in 1957. I didn't want anyone going home and saying, 'I can see why they never made the Beatles.'"

Visitors to that fête saw a handwritten sign directing them to Eleanor Rigby's grave. Eleanor had worked as a scullery maid at the local hospital. She died in 1939 at the age of forty-four, and her coffin, the third of five, is buried deep in a family grave. John and Paul were known to relax among the gravestones, as teenagers do, and the name may have stuck in Paul's subconscious.

introduce John to his musical friend, fifteen-year-old Paul McCartney. Paul's mother, Mary, had died some months earlier; now he was starting to socialize again. Ivan suggested that Paul should come to the fête. Paul went, along with his guitar. Around 6 p.m., the Quarrymen moved to the church hall to set up for the evening performance.

While they were chatting, Ivan introduced Paul to the Quarrymen. He impressed them by playing Eddie Cochran's "Twenty Flight Rock" and Gene Vincent's "Be-Bop-A-Lula." He gave them the lyrics for "Twenty Flight Rock" and showed them how to tune a guitar. "I can remember Paul doing something with his guitar, and I thought he was a show-off," go," explains Rod Davis. "The rest of the band went without me and got through the heat. Then there was the show itself, where we only played one number—'Worried Man Blues.' Another skiffle group had come from North Wales with a coachload of supporters, and they beat us on the applause meter. All credit to them, though. They were leaping all over the stage, and the bass player was rolling on his back. They gave a real show. We were just standing there, expecting people to appreciate our music."

"The last group on had an extra three minutes," says Colin. "They did two songs, and they were the winners. When Carroll Levis called us back on stage, he said, 'I might have been a bit unfair there, lads, but you were good, so keep at it.'"

ENTER THE CAVERN

Who could have predicted that a small cellar in Liverpool's fruit market would become the most famous club in the world? In the 1950s, Mathew Street in Liverpool was a narrow thoroughfare with seven-story warehouses, mostly used for fruit and vegetables, on either side. The basement of number 10 was typical: it had been an air-raid shelter in the war and then used for packing eggs. In 1956, it was empty.

Alan Sytner, the son of a local doctor, was running jazz evenings nearby at the Temple, but the venue lacked atmosphere. After visiting Le Caveau, a ten-year-old club on the Left Bank of the Seine in Paris, he knew what he was looking for, and he purchased the lease for the basement of 10 Mathew Street and called his new club the Cavern.

Punters and performers alike entered the venue through a dimly lit doorway, then went down sixteen narrow stone steps to the cellar. The Cavern was divided by archways into three areas: one for collecting admissions and acting as a cloakroom with space for dancing, a central

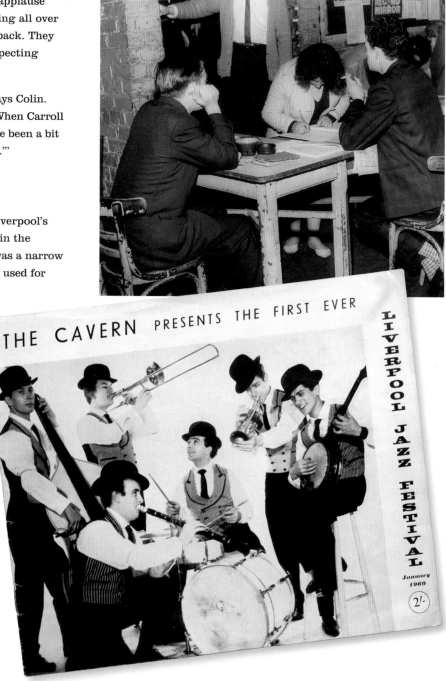

Left: Charlie McBain booked the Quarrymen for New Clubmoor Hall in Norris Green, Liverpool, on October 18, 1957, writing "Good and bad" in his notes. Nevertheless, they were rebooked for November 23, 1957, when this shot was taken.

It was a fateful night, as Colin Hanton recalls: "We played some skiffle numbers at the start, but then we moved on to some rock 'n' roll. John Lennon was passed a note, and he said to the audience, 'We've had a request.' He opened it up. Alan Sytner had written, 'Cut out the bloody rock 'n' roll.'" As a result, the Quarrymen's fee was reduced from £5 to £3 10s.

But the Quarrymen weren't the only group to rebel in the club. Ringo, who had performed at the Cavern as part of the Eddie Clayton Skiffle Group, appeared at the first Liverpool Jazz Festival, held at the Cavern in January 1960 with Rory Storm and the Hurricanes. Rory defied instructions by rampaging through "Whole Lotta Shakin' Goin' On." The Cavern's new manager, Ray McFall, docked their fee, but they made it up by collecting the hard, old pennies that the audience had thrown to show their disapproval.

Opposite: Queueing on the steep, narrow steps down into the Cavern.
Opposite, below: Program for the first Liverpool Jazz Festival at the Cavern with Acker Bilk (pictured with his band) and Terry Lightfoot.

one with a small stage and a few rows of chairs, and another area for dancing. There were no decorations, curtains, or colored lights. There was no ventilation, and on a busy night, seven hundred people would pack into the club. Condensation would drip from the walls, and nearly everyone would be smoking. The first thing you wanted after a night out at the Cavern was a shower. The members endured such a hellhole because the sound was excellent; the groups likened it to a giant echo chamber.

The Cavern had opened in January 1957 as a traditional jazz venue, and as skiffle had grown out of traditional jazz, it was acceptable as interval entertainment. Rock 'n' rollers and jazz fans were in opposing camps, and if a group played the wrong music there could be trouble. Fortunately for the Quarrymen, Alan Sytner's father belonged to the Lee Park Golf Club, where Nigel Walley was an apprentice golf pro, and Alan gave them a few guest appearances, billing them in their own right on Wednesday, August 7, 1957.

By this time Paul McCartney was in the group, but he was at Scout camp in the Lake District and missed this performance.

By the end of 1957, Len Garry left the band after being diagnosed with tuberculosis, which he could have contracted in the then unsanitary Cavern. George Harrison came into the group, and Eric and Colin drifted away. "John, Paul, and Eric Griffiths were the three guitarists," says Colin, "and I was on drums. Eventually we were playing at the Morgue club in the Old Swan district, which was run by Rory Storm. It was in a condemned terraced house, and the whole thing was illegal. The front room became a tiny dance hall with a stage. There was a long corridor to the other rooms, and that is where we met George Harrison. Somebody asked him to play something. I thought it was 'Guitar Boogie,' but everyone else reckons it was 'Raunchy.' A few days later, Ivan Vaughan told me that John and Paul wanted George to join the group, but Eric would have to go, as they didn't want four guitarists. I was living on borrowed time, as they were running the group. I got fed up. None of us had cars, and I had carted my drums around on a bus for two years. There were a lot of talent contests where we came second—we were always the bridesmaid, and I'd had enough."

3 FROM QUARRYMEN TO BEATLES

"My grandpa was the first man to record the Beatles, and it was the only record they made in Liverpool. It is quite a big thing, but his name isn't often in the books. He was a professional engineer, and he wore a brown coat and tie. He came across as an old grump to them, but he was a great guy."

PETER PHILLIPS

Left: On December 9, 1961, Sam Leach booked the Beatles into the Palais Ballroom, Aldershot, located thirty-five miles from London. Due to a lack of promotion, the Beatles' first booking down south attracted eighteen people.

Above: Percy Phillips's recording studio at 38 Kensington.
Opposite: Mona Best's son, Pete, in the Spider Room at the Casbah.

NOWADAYS THERE ARE RECORDING STUDIOS
EVERYWHERE; some readers will even have them in their
own homes. Back in the 1950s, it was very different. There
were few studios outside London, and not many in London,
for that matter, as the commercial market was dominated by
four companies: EMI, Decca, Pye, and Philips. In Liverpool,

there was a small studio owned by Percy Phillips at 38
Kensington, in an area a mile from the city center.

Percy Phillips, who was born in 1896, originally sold bicycles
and motorcycles. He had been interested in recording
technology for many years, so he opened a studio in his
back room in 1955. He recorded residents who wanted to
hear themselves sing, send Christmas messages to relatives
abroad, or impress commercial recording companies. Ken
Dodd asked Percy to record his radio appearances on disc.
The first recorded example of rock 'n' roll in Liverpool is
"She's Got It" by Johnny Guitar and Paul Murphy, cut by
Percy Phillips in 1957.

In the summer of 1958, a young Ronnie Wycherley wanted
to impress the London impresario Larry Parnes; he recorded
a two-sided 78-rpm shellac disc with Percy. He was invited
to meet Parnes when he was in Birkenhead with a touring
package starring the singer Marty Wilde, and a tour and a
Decca contract followed. (When at last the performances from
38 Kensington were officially released, young Ronnie was
instantly recognizable as Billy Fury—the stage name that
Parnes had decided Wycherley should use.)

Around the same time (probably on July 12, 1958), the
Quarrymen made a record at Percy Phillips's studio. The
lineup was John Lennon, Paul McCartney, George Harrison
(all with amplified acoustic guitars), drummer Colin Hanton,
and pianist John Duff Lowe. They each paid 3s 6d—less than
£1 in total. "That'll Be the Day" featured a decent enough
performance, with John on lead vocals, and it's appropriate
that their first recording was written by the songwriter who
inspired them the most—Buddy Holly. In fact, in March 1958
Buddy Holly and the Crickets toured the UK, appearing at the
Liverpool Philharmonic Hall on March 20. Many of the young
skiffle musicians who went to that concert saw Holly playing
a Fender Stratocaster—after that, it was no more acoustic
music for them.

The other side of the disc was an original, a country ballad,
"In Spite of All the Danger." Although written by Paul, who
had clearly been listening to Elvis Presley's "Tryin' to Get
to You," the ballad was attributed to McCartney/Harrison,

as George had contributed a guitar solo. The recording was perilously close to the three-minute barrier, the maximum time available on a disc, and Percy signaled for the band to stop. The original disc is now the most valuable recording ever, worth £100,000. The Beatles included the tracks on the first *Anthology* in 1995, the re-formed Quarrymen recorded "In Spite of All the Danger" in 2004, and Paul sang it on his U.S. tour the following year.

Each Quarryman owned the acetate for a week, and fortunately it didn't suffer too much damage. John Duff Lowe, the fifth owner of the acetate, held onto it until he sold it to Paul McCartney in 1981. John would have had the acetate for the first week, and it is possible that Mimi and Julia played it. If so, Julia would have heard John singing, "That'll be the day when I die."

Mimi usually accompanied Julia to the bus stop for her journey home, but on the fateful evening of July 15, 1958, she stayed indoors. Julia met the Quarrymen's so-called manager, Nigel Walley, who happened to be walking by, and they exchanged a few words. This was her last conversation, for as she crossed the dual carriageway she was hit by a speeding car and killed instantly.

That evening John went to visit his mother, and it was at her house that he received the devastating news. For several weeks, John retreated into himself: he didn't want to see anyone; he didn't want to talk about her; he didn't want to play music. John and Paul now had another common bond.

John was shocked when the driver of the car, an off-duty policeman, was acquitted. The Quarrymen stopped playing for a time, but they did perform in December 1958 at the wedding reception for George's brother Harry. Maybe John was uneasy at being back on the stage, as he poured a drink over one of the guests; fortunately, she didn't seem to mind. After all, Liverpool weddings can be boisterous.

In January 1959, fed up with the lack of Quarrymen gigs, George Harrison joined another local band, the Les Stewart Quartet. The group was booked for the opening of the Casbah Club in August 1959, but an argument caused the group to split up, so they did not perform. Instead, Ken Brown and George Harrison persuaded John and Paul to join them for the Casbah Club opening, and the four, billed as the Quarrymen, played several gigs there. At one date in October, Ken Brown was ill, and when Mona Best gave the Quarrymen their fee, she held back Ken's share to give him later. John, Paul, and George thought this unfair (as indeed it was), so the Quarrymen boycotted the Casbah. Ken Brown formed a new resident band, the Blackjacks, with Bill Barlow (guitar), Chas Newby (bass), and Mona's son Pete on drums.

THE CASBAH

LIVE ENTERTAINMENT WAS AN INTEGRAL PART OF LIFE IN LIVERPOOL. This passion had led, over previous decades, to the establishment of numerous venues throughout the city center and surrounding suburbs. A network of town halls, dance halls, church halls, jazz clubs, cinemas, and theaters was already available to local beat musicians. And although there was no need to create new clubs, one of the few that emerged was the Casbah in West Derby, run by the formidable Mona Best.

During the war, Donald Scanland, a marine engineer in India, married Mona Shaw (known as Mo), and they had a son, Randolph Peter Best, born in Madras on November 24, 1941. After Donald was lost at sea, Mo married a navy lieutenant,

The Casbah Coffee Club "Exclusive"

Johnny Best, who came from Liverpool. Johnny adopted Peter, and they had another son, John Rory Best, born on January 29, 1945.

The family came to Liverpool later that year, and Johnny helped his father, also called Johnny, with promoting boxing at Liverpool Stadium. In 1954 Mo sold some jewelry and put the proceeds on a horse, Never Say Die, ridden by Lester Piggott at 33 to 1 in the Epsom Derby. With her winnings and the help of a small mortgage, she bought a fifteen-room Victorian house in Haymans Green, West Derby. Mo, who later became estranged from Johnny, raised Pete and Rory in Haymans Green.

A club called Lowlands opened across the road from Mo, featuring live groups on the weekend and a jukebox during the week. Mo, who had also seen a TV documentary about coffee bars in London, was determined to open her own club. She called it the Casbah, a reference to Charles Boyer's stronghold in the 1938 film *Algiers*.

The Casbah, four miles outside of the city center, was a teenage club created exclusively for beat music. Not only did the embryo Beatles play there, but also Gerry and the Pacemakers, the Searchers, Faron's Flamingos, the Undertakers, and a Manchester band, the Dakotas.

Many teenagers helped to decorate the club, and to this day you can still see the work of the Beatles. There are more than two

hundred painted stars in one room, but who painted what? John carelessly used slow-drying gloss paint; as a result, the walls were not dry on the opening night, August 29, 1959. Admission was a shilling, and annual membership was 12/6d. Notwithstanding the proximity of Lowlands, the Casbah became a magnet for teenagers. It had over 1,000 members, but it was limited to 150 at any one time. "We did have a couple of bouncers," Mo recalled, "but the Casbah did have a very friendly atmosphere. I have never known [another] atmosphere like it."

The basement consisted of seven adjoining rooms: on the face of it, this was wrong for a beat club, as you couldn't see the band or hear the music properly. One large open space would have been preferable, but a small stage area was created, and a counter for selling coffee, snacks, and soft drinks was installed, along with some bench seating. As long as a club wasn't licensed, there were few health and safety regulations. The neighbors did not complain: they considered their children safe under Mrs. Best's supervision.

Before Mo opened the Casbah, her older son, Pete, had already shown an interest in playing the guitar, but once the Casbah opened he started to chat with the drummers. At first Pete bought a snare drum and a cymbal; soon he wanted the full kit.

The Quarrymen performed at the opening of the Casbah, and the Beatles played at its closure on June 24, 1962; by then they had played the club about fifty times. The Casbah closed as Mo was about to give birth and also because the Beatles had outgrown the small club. Because their road manager, Neil Aspinall, was still living with the Bests, the Beatles continued to store their equipment in the Casbah even after Pete's dismissal, and this continued until well into 1963.

The house has remained with the Best family, and in 1999 a plaque was unveiled to show its historical importance as "the birthplace of the Beatles." The Casbah itself reopened in August 2002 with a set from the Pete Best band. There are special events, and private tours can be arranged; your guide will be one of Mo's sons—Pete, Rory, or Roag (born in 1962).

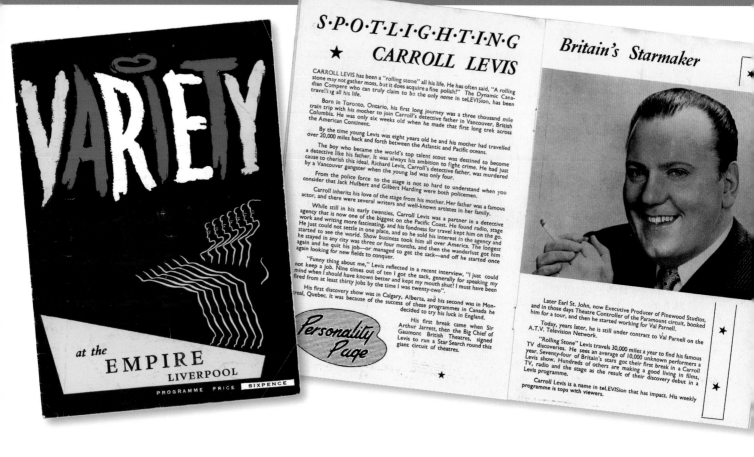

S·P·O·T·L·I·G·H·T·I·N·G
★ CARROLL LEVIS

Britain's Starmaker

CARROLL LEVIS has been a "rolling stone" all his life. He has often said, "A rolling stone may not gather moss, but it does acquire a fine polish!" The Dynamic Canadian Compere who can truly claim to be the only name in teLEVISion, has been travelling all his life.

Born in Toronto, Ontario, his first long journey was a three thousand mile train trip with his mother to join Carroll's detective father in Vancouver, British Columbia. He was only six weeks old when he made that first long trek across the American Continent.

By the time young Levis was eight years old he and his mother had travelled over 20,000 miles back and forth between the Atlantic and Pacific oceans.

The boy who became the world's top talent scout was destined to become a detective like his father. It was always his ambition to fight crime. He had just cause to cherish this ideal. Richard Levis, Carroll's detective father, was murdered by a Vancouver gangster when the young lad was only four.

From the police force to the stage is not so hard to understand when you consider that Jack Hulbert and Gilbert Harding were both policemen.

Carroll inherits his love of the stage from his mother. Her father was a famous actor, and there were several writers and well-known artistes in her family.

While still in his early twenties, Carroll Levis was a partner in a detective agency that is now one of the biggest on the Pacific Coast. He found radio, stage work and writing more fascinating, and his fondness for travel kept him on the go. He just could not settle in one place, and so he sold his interest in the agency and started to see the world. Show business took him all over America. The longest he stayed in any city was three or four months, and then the wanderlust got him again and he quit his job—or managed to get the sack—and off he started once again looking for new fields to conquer.

"Funny thing about me," Levis reflected in a recent interview, "I just could not keep a job. Nine times out of ten I got the sack, generally for speaking my mind when I should have known better and kept my mouth shut! I must have been fired from at least thirty jobs by the time I was twenty-two."

His first discovery show was in Calgary, Alberta, and his second was in Montreal, Quebec. It was because of the success of these programmes in Canada he decided to try his luck in England.

His first break came when Sir Arthur Jarrett, then the Big Chief of Gaumont British Theatres, signed Levis to run a Star Search round this giant circuit of theatres.

Personality Page

Later Earl St. John, now Executive Producer of Pinewood Studios, and in those days Theatre Controller of the Paramount circuit, booked him for a tour, and then he started working for Val Parnell.

Today, years later, he is still under contract to Val Parnell on the A.T.V. Television Network.

"Rolling Stone" Levis travels 30,000 miles a year to find his famous TV discoveries. He sees an average of 10,000 unknown performers a year. Seventy-four of Britain's stars got their first break in a Carroll Levis show. Hundreds of others are making a good living in films, TV, radio and the stage as the result of their discovery debut in a Levis programme.

Carroll Levis is a name in teLEVISion that has impact. His weekly programme is tops with viewers.

John, Paul, and George renamed themselves Johnny and the Moondogs and auditioned for Carroll Levis's TV *Star Search* at the Empire Theatre. They reached the North West final, held at the Hippodrome Theatre, Ardwick, Manchester, on November 15, 1959. They performed well but had to leave early to catch the last train. Unfortunately for them—and in something of a repeat of the June 1957 Quarrymen performance—the judging was based on applause for the reprise.

Although John, Paul, and George had not played many gigs in 1959, they had learned new material and were finding their vocal styles. Paul had developed a Little Richard voice, while John was at his best with Chuck Berry and Gene Vincent material. George went for Carl Perkins, and they all liked singing Elvis and Buddy Holly.

But they were not yet a rock 'n' roll band. They didn't have a regular drummer or a new electric bass, which at the time was replacing the bulky double bass: Rory Storm and the Hurricanes featured Lu Walters on electric bass on a stunning version of "Brand New Cadillac," and Rory gave his drummer, Richard Starkey, his own spot, Ringo Starr-Time. The Hurricanes were more professional than the Quarrymen but more of a show band, as Rory favored novelty rock 'n' roll songs like "Splish Splash" and "Lend Me Your Comb."

The new electric bass would be supplied by someone who didn't know how to play it, someone who met John Lennon as a fellow pupil at Liverpool College of Art in 1957—Stu Sutcliffe.

ART AND ARTISTS

The Liverpool College of Art was on Hope Street, close to the Anglican cathedral and next to Liverpool Institute—indeed, part of the same building. In the 1950s and '60s, the art colleges in the various cities were bohemian strongholds. They encouraged individual thinking and creativity, but they also appealed to those who were talented but not disciplined enough to study for a university degree. It was not just

Above: Liverpool College of Art with the Liverpool Institute to the right.
Opposite: Program for Carroll Levis's *TV Star Search* at Liverpool Empire in October 1959. John, Paul, and George took part as Johnny and the Moondogs, while Ringo Starr was in Jett (later Rory) Storm and the Hurricanes. Lennon's group got through to the final.

a coincidence that many of the '60s top rock stars—John Lennon, Ray Davies, Pete Townshend, Eric Burdon—had an art school education. "You could get by with very little real work," says Pete Frame, the creator of Rock Family Trees. "You could get your posters done for nothing, you could live on an art school grant, and you could rehearse in school facilities."

During the 1950s in Britain, there was a clear divide in the education system for the masses (excluding the private fee-paying schools). On one side of the divide, "grammar" schools were open to all, but entrance was selective in favor of the academically bright. These students were more likely to listen to jazz and classical music and take an interest in the political news of the day. On the other side was "secondary" education, for the mainstream teenager who was nonacademic and interested in the sounds of rock 'n' roll. Although higher education establishments theoretically accepted students from all economic backgrounds, the selection process for universities favored those from grammar schools. Art colleges

offered a far more flexible selection process. Not only did this provide access to further education to students who would otherwise have been lost to the system, but it also created a rich hybrid of cultures with students who came from a wide range of backgrounds.

"From the social melting pot of the grammar schools," writes Mike Evans in *The Lennon Companion*, "came a mixed bag of cultural references: kids from terraced back streets more interested in pulp comics than Picasso; suburban romantics hung up on the new Beat writers; and everywhere the all-pervasive influence of rock 'n' roll and the English skiffle craze that went with it. The result was a species of which the seventeen-year-old John Lennon was both typical and one of the first—the art-student-as-Teddy-Boy."

Top and top, right: Ye Cracke pub, near the art college. In 1958 Stu and Rod painted a mural in the back room and John was temporarily banned for mocking one of the regulars. The picture on the right shows a performance with Adrian Henri (standing center) and Mike Hart (standing right).
Center: Stu Sutcliffe in Percy Street, 1959. Adrian Henri said, "Stu's posthumous reputation doesn't need the glamour of his former band to enhance it."
Above: The art college on Hope Street in 1957.

It was against this cultural backdrop that John Lennon, as a new student in September 1957, joined the introductory course in lettering at the Liverpool College of Art. And it was here that he met Cynthia Powell, later to be Cynthia Lennon, as well as his close friends Stuart Sutcliffe, Rod Murray, and Bill Harry. The four boys would drink in a nearby pub, Ye Cracke, and determine how they would change the world—one as a musician, two as artists, and one as a magazine editor. They called themselves the Dissenters, and today a plaque in the Ye Cracke pub acknowledges this group of influential friends.

"There are rebellious spirits in any college of art, and that is a very good thing," explained Nicholas Horsfield, painter and lecturer at Liverpool College of Art. "I had to try to teach Lennon objective life drawing. Life drawing is an essential core discipline in learning to be a painter. It involves observation and analysis, feeling, expression, and this sort of thing was sheer nonsense to John. I was never able to get him to concentrate at all in the actual study of the model. I soon gave up trying. I would leave Lennon to doodle on his own until he chose to walk out."

June Furlong, who was a life model at the college, remembers John as "a Liverpool lad stinking of fish and chips." "I liked him a lot," she says, "I had been to London, and he wanted to talk about all the artists that I knew, like Lucian Freud. He did disrupt the class from time to time, and people would say, 'Shut up and get on with your drawing.' He loved the comedian Robb Wilton, and he could do a great impersonation of him."

Although John Lennon was a troublemaker at the college, he had respect for the tutor Arthur Ballard, who spotted the potential in Stuart Sutcliffe and John. Stuart preferred to work in his flat in Percy Street, and Arthur would give him personal tuition. "Arthur knew that John was disruptive," says Bill Harry, "but he liked him and wanted to help him out. A new graphic art department was being started at the college, and Arthur recommended that

John and I become the first students. They accepted me, but they turned down John because of his reputation. Arthur would go over to Ye Cracke pub with the students, and he was really helpful, plus he was a great artist in his own right."

In the summer of 1959, Stuart and Rod decided to submit a painting to the biennial John Moores Exhibition of modern art at the city's Walker Art Gallery. "Of his year," commented Nicholas Horsfield, "Stuart Sutcliffe was the most dedicated and potentially the most able, the one who worked much harder and more productively than anyone else." Stuart's was a large work on two boards, so Rod and Stuart delivered the first half, but on the way back to collect the second they became sidetracked in Ye Cracke pub—and the remaining half was never delivered. "There were 2,500 entries, including one from Arthur Ballard," explains Bill Harry. "Arthur's was turned down, but Stuart's was accepted for the Exhibition, and John Moores bought the painting. But Stu didn't use the money to buy the bass guitar; the one he got at Frank Hessy's was on hire purchase [paid for in installments]."

The importance of having a picture in the John Moores Exhibition is evident in the art school pantomime *Cinderella*, written by Rod, Stu, and John and staged in December 1959. Cinderella (Ella in the script, and played by their friend June Harry, Bill's cousin) has a painting accepted for the John Moores Exhibition, but her ugly sisters Hortense and Gwyn, played by John Lennon and his friend Geoff Mohammed, won't allow Ella to attend the Private View. "But I wanted to be terribly arty and make the people think I'm a beatnikker," says a lamenting Ella to Buttons. The script contains many plays on words and references to "cripples," a Lennon fixation.

As the Liverpool Institute was next door to the art college, Paul—who was studying for his A-levels—and George could meet regularly with John and Stuart. By 1959, the favored music at the art school had moved from jazz to rock 'n' roll, and Lennon saw an opportunity for playing at student dances held at the college.

Top: Stu Sutcliffe with one of his paintings hanging over the fireplace at Percy Street, 1959.
Above: Annual cricket match between the art college's lecturers and students. Arthur Ballard, tutor and mentor to both John and Stuart, is second left, and Rod Murray, looking to camera, is eighth from the left.

John Lennon had mentioned to both Rod and Stu, independently, that he was looking for a bass guitar (and bass guitarist) for the group. Rod was in the process of making a bass guitar when Stu bought his Hofner President from Frank Hessy's. "Stuart had a Hofner bass guitar, which was the bee's knees, but he couldn't play a note," recalls fellow art college student Dave May of the Silhouettes. "I remember going over to John and Stuart's flat. I said, 'I'll teach you to play "C'mon Everybody" if you let me measure your guitar.' I taught him to play the song—it's only three notes. I then measured his guitar so I could make my own, and Stu Sutcliffe played with the Beatles."

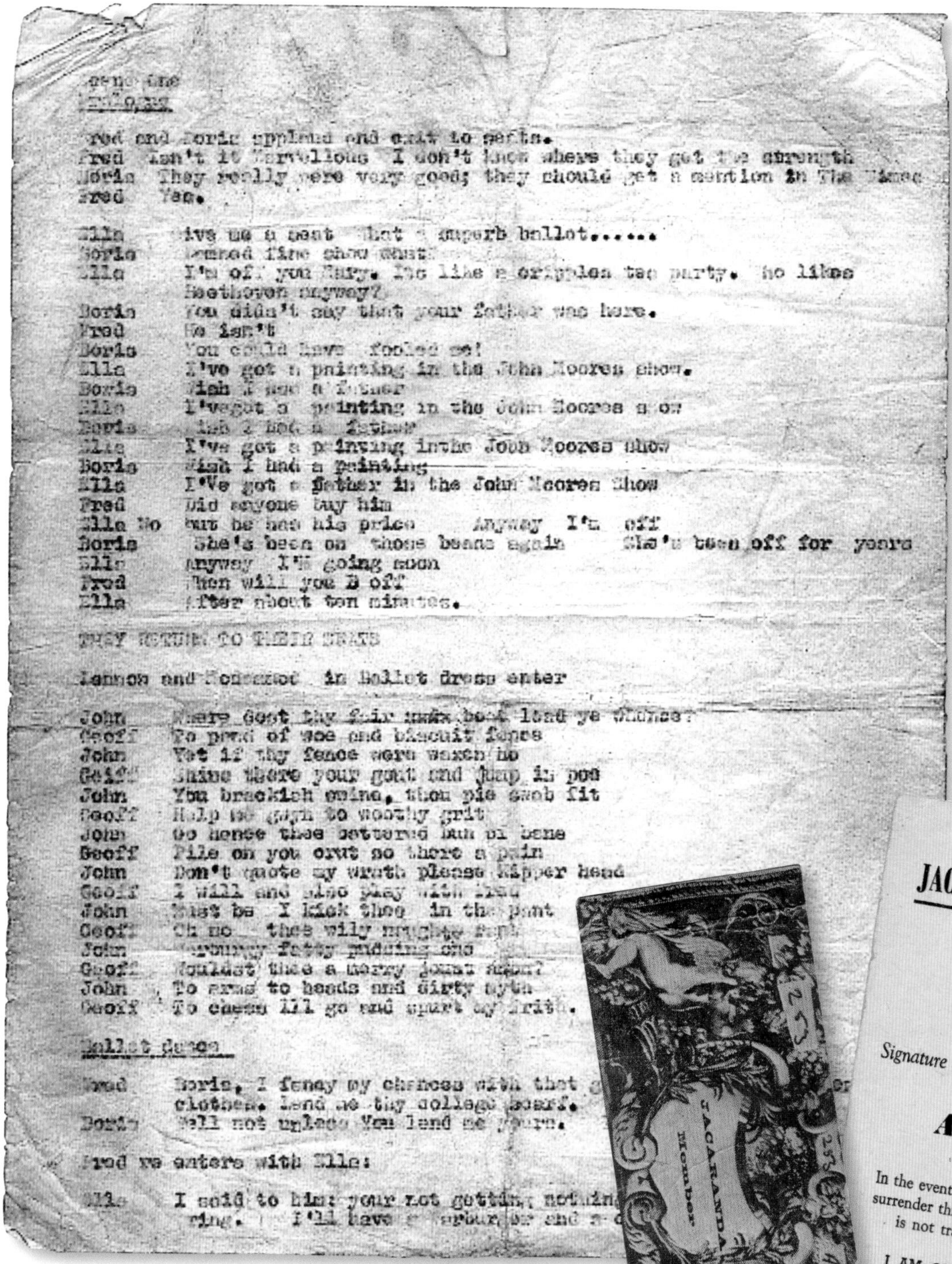

Left: A page from the script of the 1959 Christmas art school pantomine, *Cinderella*, written by John, Stuart, and Rod. It references the inclusion of one of Stuart's paintings in the prestigious John Moores Exhibition at the Walker Art Gallery. John and Geoff were the ugly sisters, and Rod played Boris (Dandini in the traditional version).

Below: Membership cards for Allan Williams's Jacaranda Club.

Opposite, top: The Jacaranda on Slater Street. Plenty of historical memorabilia remain on its walls.

Opposite, below: The flyer for the Eddie Cochran and Gene Vincent concert at Liverpool Stadium had to be quickly amended and reprinted after Cochran's death in April 1960.

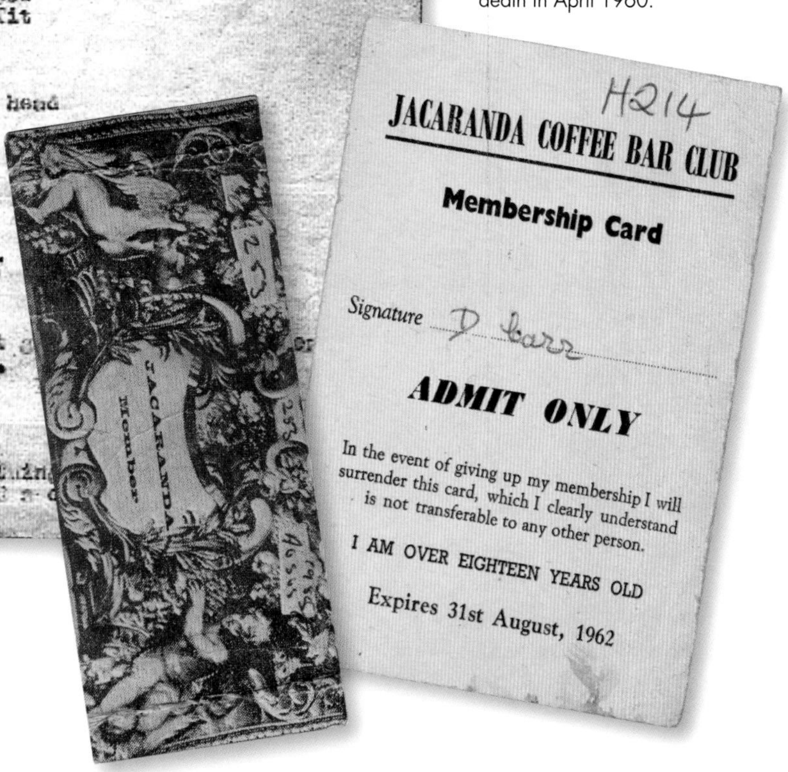

JACARANDA COFFEE BAR CLUB

H214

Membership Card

Signature *D Carr*

ADMIT ONLY

In the event of giving up my membership I will surrender this card, which I clearly understand is not transferable to any other person.

I AM OVER EIGHTEEN YEARS OLD

Expires 31st August, 1962

In January 1960, Stu joined John, Paul, and George in the Quarrymen—which Stu renamed the Beatals [sic], followed by the Silver Beetles—with a view to playing regularly at the Friday afternoon dances in the Students' Union. As the group did not have enough amplifiers, they asked the Students' Union to buy one. Providentially, both Stu and Bill Harry were on the Entertainments Committee, and an amplifier was purchased with the proviso that it should never leave the building. It did, and the Beatles were to use it, off and on, until 1962.

One of the Beatles' haunts was Allan Williams's Jacaranda coffee bar in Slater Street. When Allan saw Eddie Cochran and Gene Vincent at the Empire in March 1960, he suggested to their agent, Larry Parnes, that they put together a big beat show with Cochran and Vincent at an unlikely venue—Liverpool Stadium.

A handbill was printed and tickets sold, but Cochran was killed in a car crash on the way back from Bristol to London. "I was shattered by the death of Eddie Cochran," says Allan Williams. "Gene Vincent was also badly hurt, and I phoned Larry Parnes and said, 'I take it for granted that it's all over.' He said, 'No. Gene Vincent has gone back to the States, but he's returning to England and would like to do it.' I put on Liverpool groups to supplement the show—Rory Storm and the Hurricanes, Bob Evans and the Five Shillings, and Cass and the Cassanovas. My friend Bob Wooler suggested Gerry and the Pacemakers, so I went to Blair Hall and was knocked out by them, and so we went ahead with the first ever Merseybeat rock 'n' roll concert." Parnes also included the Liverpool acts Lance Fortune and Mal Perry.

The stadium show took place on May 3, 1960, and although historically significant, it was hampered by poor sound and bad organization. Nevertheless, John, Paul, and George were annoyed that Allan Williams had not considered them good enough to appear. "The stadium was a strange place to play," says Fred Marsden, drummer with the Pacemakers. "The sound got lost."

"The stadium show was a total madhouse," says rock 'n' roll aficionado Mick O'Toole, who went to the performance to see what Liverpool bands could do. "With its seating, the

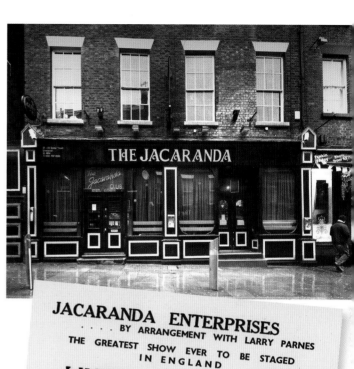

JACARANDA ENTERPRISES
· · · · BY ARRANGEMENT WITH LARRY PARNES
THE GREATEST SHOW EVER TO BE STAGED
IN ENGLAND

LIVERPOOL STADIUM
Tuesday, May 3rd at 8 p.m.
(THREE HOUR PROGRAMME)   DOORS OPEN 7-30 P.M.

GENE VINCENT

Davy Jones
ITALY'S NERO AND HIS GLADIATORS
with the fabulous NEW SOUND from Italy

Lance Fortune
PYE HIT PARADE, "BE MINE"

Peter Wynne   Julian X

The Viscounts

Colin Green
AND THE BEAT BOYS

Billy Raymond
YOUR HOST & COMPERE

PLUS Liverpool's CASS AND THE CASSANOVAS
RORY STORM AND THE HURRICANES
JERRY AND THE PACEMAKERS
MAL PERRY AND RICKY LEA
JOHNNY & THE JETS   DERRY & THE SENIORS

PRICES: — 10/- — 7/6d. — 5/- — 3/6d.
Tickets available from Lewis's, Cranes, Rushworth's, Beaver Radio, Frank Hessy, The Stadium, Top Hat Record Bar, Dale St., the Jacaranda Coffee Bar, and Nem's.

ARTISTS AND POETS

The Beat Generation encompassed poets, artists, and musicians. And it was inevitable that Liverpool Art College would become a catalyst for the city's own bohemian beatnik scene. Groups of musicians, poets, writers, and artists bonded over drinks at coffee bars, clubs, and pubs such as Ye Cracke, the Philharmonic pub, Picasso Club, and the Jacaranda.

"We used to obtain poetry books from the City Lights bookshop in San Francisco. John liked a poem by Lawrence Ferlinghetti called 'Christ Climbed Down.' I would walk down the street reciting Allen Ginsberg's 'Howl.'"

BILL HARRY

"I recall meeting George Harrison in the Jacaranda, and I went to the Gambier Terrace flat, where I stayed for a while. It was there where I met the embryo Beatles, as George and Paul used to visit John."

ROYSTON ELLIS, POET AND AUTHOR

Left: Adrian Henri with his art work, mid-'60s. The large packet of soap powder indicates Andy Warhol's influence, while the main painting is *The Entry of Christ into Liverpool* (1964), inspired by James Ensor's *The Entry of Christ into Brussels in 1889* (1888), which was also an influence on Peter Blake's album cover for *Sgt. Pepper.*

"When I was seventeen or eighteen, poetry belonged to some sort of academic elite, and then suddenly it was discovered that you could write poetry for yourself and entertain and amuse your friends. It became a public expression, and the same thing applies to song lyrics. A lot of people were against it. The painters at the art college felt that what we were doing was a load of rubbish, and little fights were breaking out all the time. I remember the poets versus the painters in Hope Hall one night. I know that George and Paul came to a couple of our events, but I don't think John came. It's one of those Liverpool things, you know. If you're sensitive, you don't want to admit it."

ROGER MCGOUGH, MEMBER OF SCAFFOLD

"Around 1961, I was looking in the *Liverpool Echo* and saw this small ad that said, 'Meet Pete the Beat at Streates,' which was a coffee bar in Liverpool. I was on the verge of leaving school, and I went to this basement coffee bar, a dark and grubby little place, but it was quite wonderful. I met Roger McGough and Adrian Henri there, and I started a magazine called *Underdog* when I was fifteen."

BRIAN PATTEN

Above: Brian Patten's poems, collected in *Little Johnny's Confession* (1967) and *Notes to the Hurrying Man* (1969), were a revelation. The *Library Journal* (USA) said the poems presented "a remarkable portrait of the bewilderment of an urbanized generation."

"I ran the film society at the art college, and we booked *Ashes and Diamonds*, a Polish film from 1958. In the film, there is a character played by the actor Zbigniew Cybulski, who wears sunglasses throughout. Stuart decided to wear dark glasses like him. He wasn't trying to look like James Dean at all."

BILL HARRY

"I remember Stuart very vividly. He had this faithful companion who was always a couple of places behind him and never said very much, rather like the Duke of Edinburgh with the Queen. That was John Lennon. In view of his later capacity for talking, it's extraordinary that I should remember him that way."

ADRIAN HENRI

"Poetry and jazz was an obscene contradiction in terms. It worked on me like a crucifix on a vampire. I ignored it in any manifestation."

STEVE VOCE, LIVERPOOL JAZZ WRITER

THE LIVERPOOL SCENE

Above: In 1965 Allen Ginsberg (left) came to London for a poetry reading at the Royal Albert Hall and poet Pete Brown brought him to Liverpool. Here he shares a bench in Liverpool's Sefton Park with Adrian Henri.

The relationship and collaboration between the Liverpool poets and the Merseybeat musicians was so integral to the cultural landscape of the period that in 1967 Edward Lucie-Smith edited a book of poetry and photographs entitled *The Liverpool Scene*, which he dedicated "To the Beatles without whom &c."

As with the musicians, the poets were heavily influenced by American culture. The genesis of the Liverpool poets lay in San Francisco's Beat scene, and Adrian Henri's style was close to that of Allen Ginsberg, who visited Liverpool in 1965, calling it "the center of the consciousness of the human universe." This was scarcely a revelation, and anyway, he made similar remarks about Prague and San Francisco. Just as Merseybeat musicians covered songs by Chuck Berry and Little Richard, many of the Liverpool poets wrote their own versions of "Beat" poetry. Henri's best-known poem, "Tonight at Noon," took its title from a Charles Mingus LP.

Roger McGough, Adrian Henri, and Brian Patten dominated the early years of the Liverpool poetry scene and created the atmosphere in which poetry could flourish. The three poets presented an intriguing mix of content and performance styles: Roger McGough had a high-speed delivery and wit, Adrian Henri's poems were lyrical and autobiographical, and Brian Patten's poetry combined a traditional romanticism with a modern cutting edge.

Adrian Henri, who had graduated from Durham University in 1955, became an art teacher and settled in the bohemian district, Liverpool 8. In 1960 he attended poetry and jazz evenings at Streates coffee bar, organized by Johnny Byrne and featuring performers from outside the area—notably Pete Brown, who became a lyricist for Cream. Henri met a fellow graduate and teacher, Roger McGough, and a young reporter, Brian Patten, and they became the nucleus of a local poetry scene. Their *modus operandi* was different from that of past generations of poets, as their work was written primarily for performance.

McGough's wit and bite rivaled John Lennon's: he was an inventive wordsmith and far more prolific, and he did, after all, write some of John's one-liners for the film *Yellow Submarine* (1968). Henri was a creative whirlwind, organizing one event after another. In the early '60s, he devised the Liverpool One Fat Lady All Electric Show, a mixed-media event that also involved McGough, John Gorman, and Paul McCartney's brother, Mike, who performed at Hope Hall—then an art cinema and basement club, now the Everyman Theatre.

The Penguin Modern Poets series had a best seller with its anthology *The Mersey Sound* (1967), which featured the work of Henri, McGough, and Patten; sales topped half a million. However, even that figure is swamped when compared to the earlier success of John Lennon's books of wordplay in verse and prose, *In His Own Write* (1964) and *A Spaniard in the Works* (1965), both strongly influenced by Lewis Carroll, *The Goon Show*, and the comedian Stanley Unwin.

Taking his lead from avant-garde artists in California and New York, such as Allan Kaprow and Yoko Ono, Henri organized Happenings—largely improvised theatrical events—in the city, two of which took place at the Cavern. However, Scouse humor was never far away—during Yoko Ono's Happening at the Bluecoat Chambers in 1967—when, as part of the performance, Ono was wrapped in bandages—John Gorman called out, "You're wanted on the phone."

Left and below: The front and reverse of Stuart's postcard home from Fraserburgh, on the Scottish tour supporting Johnny Gentle: "Going like a bomb, love every minute, Scotland beautiful here particularly. See you Monday—I hope. Luck [sic] after yourself. Stuart."

stadium wasn't set out like the Empire, and people were dashing about all over the place. There were no marshals or stewards and no discipline among the crowds. It was a very unsettled night. There was a difference in attitude. If you went to the Empire, you behaved yourself, but this was a boxing stadium, and it was a shambles."

At the event, Parnes told Williams that he was looking for a touring band to accompany Billy Fury and that Fury would feel comfortable with Liverpool lads. Williams arranged an audition at the Wyvern Club, 108 Seel Street, around the corner from the Jacaranda, on May 10, and both Fury and Parnes attended. John, Paul, George, and Stu asked Tommy Moore to play drums, but he arrived late, so Johnny Hutchinson from Cass and the Cassanovas stood in. Parnes didn't consider them good enough for Fury but offered them a week's work backing Johnny Gentle on a Scottish tour.

SILVER BEETLES TO THE BEATLES

Billed as "Johnny Gentle and his group," the Silver Beetles—John, Paul, George, and Stuart, with Tommy

Moore on drums—went on a week's tour in Scotland (May 20–28, 1960). The group performed at Alloa, Inverness, Fraserburgh, Keith, Forres, Nairn, and Peterhead. While traveling between venues, Gentle asked Lennon to help out on a song he was writing, "I've Just Fallen for Someone." Lennon supplied the bridge, which owed something to Barrett Strong's "Money." "I've Just Fallen for Someone" was recorded by Adam Faith (1961) and by Gentle himself as Darren Young (1962), and it is the first recorded example of a John Lennon lyric, albeit the song was solely credited to John Askew (Gentle's real name). During the tour Tommy Moore suffered minor injuries in a road accident and bore the brunt of John Lennon's sarcasm. Although Gentle reported back that the

Silver Beetles were performing well in their own spot, Parnes did not give them further bookings.

Upon their return to Liverpool, Tommy Moore quit the band; his girlfriend informed John, Paul, George, and Stuart of his steady job at Garston Bottle Works, and John Lennon did not return to the art college. It is quite likely that he would have been thrown out for not working anyway. "He would never have made it as an artist," said Nicholas Horsfield. "In the visual field he would never had had the depth of expression that he had within music. As far as John Lennon was concerned, the art school gave him a year or two to relax and find himself."

The Silver Beetles (which very quickly became the Silver Beatles) had three regular venues on Merseyside. They performed in the cramped basement of the Jacaranda coffee bar, at the Neston Institute, and in the Grosvenor Ballroom, Liscard. In July, Johnny Gentle was visiting home and joined them on stage at the Grosvenor. They had a new drummer, Norman Chapman, a picture framer from an art shop opposite the Jacaranda.

"Paul McCartney had heard me practicing in the workshop," said Norman, "and he asked me to sit in at the Jac. There were no rehearsals, but it was fairly easy, twelve-bar blues and stuff like that. I wanted to play with a group, and it was fine. However, I was newly married and twenty-two and one of the last to be conscripted. I was in the King's Regiment in Kenya when it was all happening for them. Sometime later, I met Ringo Starr in the White House pub, and I was keeping time on the bar with two pennies. Ringo said, 'You keep tempo pretty good. Who have you been playing with?' I said, 'Well, I did play with the Beatles.'"

Not only did Norman not last long with the Beatles, but the dances at the Grosvenor were stopped. Liverpool Corporation (the Council) withdrew the license because of hooliganism. "There was a lot of fighting at the Grosvenor," Norman recalled, "We continued playing while the police were dragging the offenders outside and turfing them onto the lawn."

"John Lennon had a tough macho image, but he shied away from fighting," remembers Bill Harry. "When the Quarrymen were at the Rosebery Street parade, John fled from a couple

Above: "Beatnik Horror" at Gambier Terrace. John and Allan Williams are on the left, with Rod Murray sitting next to the fireplace. "Most Beatniks like dirt. They dress in filthy clothes. Their 'homes' are strewn with muck. This, for example, is the flat of a Beatnik group in Liverpool. The man on the extreme left, Allen [sic] Williams, is a little out of place in these surroundings. He is the only one who is not a beatnik and who dresses in clean clothes," wrote the *People*. Guests sometimes slept in the bath and John and Stu burned furniture to keep warm, both incidents finding their way into "Norwegian Wood." The article in the *People*, combined with complaints of "noise," contributed to the landlord's agent issuing a final eviction notice. By this point, however, John and Stu were in Hamburg.

Right: A rare photo booth picture of John from 1960. On the reverse he wrote, "Me Cross-Eyed."

of thugs and ran into somebody's house. Then again at Wilson Hall, two thugs ran after him. John got on the bus, and they beat the bus to the next stop and jumped on. He was terrified, but while they were searching the top deck, he jumped off."

By early 1960, John was sharing digs with Stuart and Rod at Gambier Terrace. John and Stuart lived in a large room at the back of the house, which was also a communal studio where on occasion the group would practice. By July, Allan Williams and his associate, the colorful Lord Woodbine, had opened a strip club in Liverpool called New Cabaret Artistes. It was soon closed (because Williams did not have a license), but not before the Silver Beatles had spent a week backing the well-endowed Janice from Manchester. They accompanied a poet from London, Royston Ellis, for his "rocketry" (poetry + rock) at the Jacaranda. "John bombarded me with questions about the London scene," Royston recalled. "I mentioned that the latest thing was to buy a Vick inhaler, open it up, and chew the wadding inside. That was a minor high compared to now."

Ever willing to search out the latest threat from society's youth, a journalist at the *People* newspaper ran an article on the bohemian subculture of beatniks that was "spreading" across the UK. An exposé, "This Is Beatnik Horror—For though they don't know it they are on the road to hell," appeared in the *People* on July 24, 1960; it reported that "this bizarre new cult imported from America is a dangerous menace to our young people."

Rod Murray recalls, "The press came to Ye Cracke and said that they were from the *Empire News*. They were concerned about students' grants and wanted to know how students managed on such small amounts of money, and could they come to our flat and see how we lived. They bought us a crate of beer, and we took them 'round. Never once did they reveal they were doing a survey of beatniks." Aunt Mimi would have been horrified to see John's photo in the article, but in all probability she never saw the *People*, as she would have regarded it as an inferior, low-quality newspaper.

After Allan Williams visited the licentious St. Pauli area of Hamburg and met the owner of the Indra and the Kaiserkeller, Bruno Koschmider, he agreed to supply Liverpool bands in exchange for a commission. He was limited in his choices,

as most band members had full-time day jobs. In the summer of 1960, Derry and the Seniors had a residency at the Kaiserkeller; the Beatles followed at the Indra. The contract called for five musicians—effectively, John, Paul, George, Stu, and a drummer. John Lennon was quoted in the 1995 *Anthology* TV series as saying, "We got Pete Best just because we needed a drummer for Hamburg." The implication is that Pete Best was a stopgap solution.

This uncharitable view was strengthened in October 2011 by the discovery of a letter from Paul McCartney responding to a classified ad in the *Liverpool Echo* that read "Drummer, young, free." He wrote on August 12, 1960, that they needed a drummer for Hamburg immediately—"If interested, ring Jacaranda club"—and the letter was signed, "Paul McCartney of the Beatles"—their latest and final stage name.

Nothing came of it (although the letter was sold for £34,000 at auction in 2011), so the Beatles with Pete Best started at the Indra on August 17 and moved to the larger Kaiserkeller on October 4. The Beatles were playing in the uninhibited St. Pauli area, and it was an astonishing way for them to grow up. They added to the mayhem by playing as excitingly as possible, and for a while, at least, Pete Best was fine. They met the maverick rock 'n' roll singer and guitarist Tony Sheridan, who encouraged them not to try and copy their favorite records: better to work out your own arrangements.

A new teenage audience came to see the Beatles in St. Pauli, but the group fell out with Koschmider: George Harrison was sent home for being underage, and Paul and Pete were deported for allegedly trying to burn down their sleeping quarters. John followed them home, while Stu stayed in Hamburg with his girlfriend, Astrid Kirchherr. Back in Liverpool in December 1960, the Beatles didn't know if they would be allowed to return to Hamburg, and they had no local gigs in their diaries.

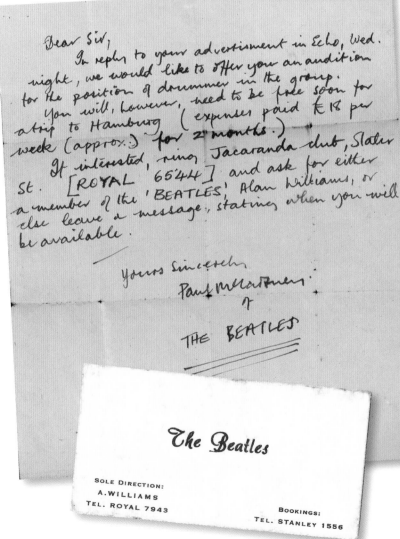

Above: Paul, John (in typical Goon form), Cavern owner Ray McFall, and Cynthia in the Cavern.
Opposite, top: Stuart (third from left) and Rod (far right) with friends in Ye Cracke.
Opposite, center: The recently discovered letter written by Paul responding to a small advert in the *Liverpool Echo*, 1960.
Opposite, bottom: Allan Williams's business card, 1960.

65

DECEMBER 27, 1960: LITHERLAND TOWN HALL

"This was the first time I heard a drummer playing fours on a bass drum. It was a wall of sound, and these were the days before you had your big PAs. They did rock 'n' roll stuff just like the Americans, but with more rawness and in a Liverpool accent. There was no way we could follow them effectively with our tinny sound."

JOHN MCNALLY, THE SEARCHERS

SINCE MAY 1959, A SOUND ENGINEER, BRIAN KELLY, HAD been promoting dances as BeeKay Promotions in the northern suburbs of Liverpool. They usually featured three beat groups and an MC, Bob Wooler. Wooler, an office worker on the docks railway, had a clear-cut delivery with succinct turns of phrase. He invented soubriquets for the performers (Rory Storm was "Mr. Showmanship," and the Remo Four "the Fender Men"), and he called himself "Mr. Big Beat." Wooler became a key figure, offering advice to aspiring bands about contracts, stage presentation, and repertoire.

Brian Kelly had organized a dance at Litherland Town Hall on Hatton Hill Road, eight miles north of Liverpool. Like many civic buildings, the hall could be hired for dancing, and as it had seen better days, Kelly relieved its shabbiness by placing Christmas

trees on the stage for his dance on December 27, 1960. He had booked Johnny Sandon with the Searchers, the Del-Renas, and the Deltones. Admission was three shillings, and if all went well, he would net £10 profit.

The Beatles were desperate to play on Merseyside. They had outgrown the Jacaranda, but they did play the Casbah as a favor to Mona Best. Bob Wooler, who hadn't heard their new sound, recommended them to Brian Kelly. Kelly was unsure: after all, they had been billed for Lathom Hall in nearby Seaforth for May 21, but the band had ignored the booking and gone to Scotland with Johnny Gentle instead. Bob was convincing; they were given a half-hour spot for £5, and they brought in Chas Newby from Pete Best's previous band, the Blackjacks, on bass.

Brian Kelly added to the poster, "Direct from Hamburg, The Beatles." It is likely that the audience thought that this was a German band at first, although their origins would have been self-evident as soon as they spoke. The Beatles had worked out their new style in Hamburg, but they didn't know how it would be accepted back home.

The effect was galvanizing, not only for the audience but also for fellow musicians. "We thought we were near the top of the heap, and we were popular around Liverpool," recalled Johnny Sandon of the Searchers. "Gerry and the Pacemakers was the leading group, and we weren't far behind. We were copying Cliff Richard and the Shadows, but the Beatles were doing something new."

Unlike other Liverpool bands with neat matching outfits, the Beatles performed in leather jackets and jeans; they even smoked on stage. Paul McCartney launched into Little Richard's "Long Tall Sally," and the audience stopped dancing and crammed forward

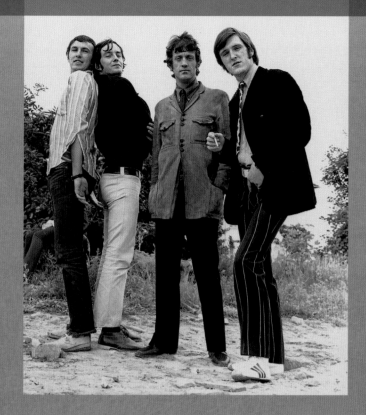

they had created in Hamburg. The Beatles could sense that they had something different and that they now had a ready-made audience. The night in Litherland was, in its own small way, a manifestation of Beatlemania.

Brian Kelly kept working with beat groups, and until his death in 1993 he ran the company, Alpha Sound in Crosby, that provided PA systems for many of the gigs in the area. There are no longer dances at Litherland Town Hall; the building was later converted into a medical center.

to watch him scream. The Beatles performed with pile-driving energy, as though their very lives depended on it.

"The place went bananas," recalled Bobby Thomson from the Dominoes. "I've never seen a reaction like it. You could sense that they were going to be big, and I wanted them to be big. You can understand hero worship from girls, but the blokes felt the same. Everybody loved them."

But not everybody approved of what they heard. "We were shocked that they commanded such a following when they looked dirty and made such a horrible, deafening row," says Don Andrew of the Remo Four. "We were intent on making our guitars sound as nice as possible, and Colin Manley was changing his strings religiously. He got a real Fender sound out of his guitar, and they came along with a big throbbing noise."

Their performance was the stuff that screams were made of, and Brian Kelly gave them further bookings, including several at Litherland Town Hall. Much to Kelly's annoyance, a rival promoter, Dave Forshaw, added some more dates.

If Paul McCartney is asked about his most memorable gig, he will cite Litherland Town Hall on December 27, 1960—placing it above Carnegie Hall and Shea Stadium. It was significant because the audience was reacting so positively to the style

Opposite: Brian Kelly, a sound engineer and part-time promoter, who added the Beatles to a beat show at Litherland Town Hall on December 27, 1960.
Above, left: Liverpool's Fender Men, the Remo Four in 1966 with Colin Manley, whom McCartney called the best guitarist in Liverpool. They had a residency at the Star-Club and also backed many of Epstein's acts on tour. From left to right: Phil Rogers, Tony Ashton, Colin Manley, and Roy Dyke.
Above: The Searchers, the Liverpool group that Epstein wanted but couldn't have. (From left to right) Chris Curtis, John McNally, Tony Jackson, and Mike Pender.

SOUP AND SWEAT AND ROCK 'N' ROLL

UNDER THE OWNERSHIP OF ALAN SYTNER, THE CAVERN HAD started lunchtime sessions for office workers, and this innovation came into its own with the new owner Ray McFall's beat sessions. You could spend an hour listening to beat music with soup, a bread roll, and a Coke. Many musicians had day jobs and couldn't play lunchtimes, so the Beatles and Gerry and the Pacemakers often shared the week's bookings.

The Beatles played their first lunchtime session at the Cavern on February 9, 1961, but Ray McFall had some reservations. Bob Wooler recalled, "Ray McFall didn't like the Beatles playing in jeans. It spelled trouble in his book, and he said to me, 'You

know the policy at the Cavern; I don't allow people in with jeans, so they can't play in them.' I groaned, as I didn't want to tell them. I knew that John would say, 'Who the fuck is he to tell us what to wear?' I asked Ray to tell them himself. He put on his pained expression, which meant 'Aren't you capable of doing it yourself?' He went into the dressing-room, and I waited for him to come out. There were no four-letter words then, as he was the guy with the pay packet." Not that the Beatles changed their appearance.

Members were treated to three local groups in the evening sessions. There was no alcohol, though some could have been

smuggled in from the Grapes pub on the opposite side of Mathew Street. Today no club could survive without an alcohol license, but it worked in the early '60s, as fans went for the music. By way of contrast, Ray McFall booked the Royal Iris ferry for occasional, very drunken Riverboat Shuffles, and the Beatles played one in August 1961 with Acker Bilk and his Paramount Jazz Band.

Freda Kelly, a Cavern regular who would later run the Beatles fan club, recalls: "I loved John singing 'Anna' and Paul doing 'Besame Mucho,' and I used to shout up for them. I don't know if they ever went out on stage with a running order, but even if

Left: Cilla Black with her best friend Pat Davies sitting on the bandstand at the Cavern, circa 1962. The drummer in the background is possibly Bobby Scott, who played with Clay and the Classics. Bobby Scott joined the Clayton Squares when they formed in late 1963.
Center: Gerry and the Pacemakers at the Cavern, 1961. Left to right: Les Chadwick, Gerry Marsden, Fred Marsden, and Les Maguire. Little Richard told Gerry, "One day you're gonna be a star, but at the moment, you're a little light bulb."
Above: Paul McCartney sitting down to play bass at the Cavern, December 8, 1961. The Beatles were backing Davy Jones, a black rock 'n' roll singer they had met in Hamburg.

BOB WOOLER
Dee Jay Compere
THE CAVERN
Liverpool
Tel Central 1591

they did, they never stayed with it, as people would shout out for things, and they would play them."

The Beatles played the Cavern about 275 times (the number depends on whether you count the Quarrymen appearances, and some dates may be unknown); their final appearance was on August 3, 1963. In January 1964 small pieces of the Cavern stage, so-called "Beatle-board," were sold for charity.

The roughest and the most raucous group on Merseyside, the Big Three, recorded the powerful "Cavern Stomp" as well as a live EP at the Cavern, and they were featured alongside both local and national bands on the Decca album *At the Cavern*. If you listen to the album, admire the carefully crafted introductions of the Cavern's DJ, Bob Wooler, who calls the club "the best of cellars."

The downfall of the Cavern lay in its hygiene. Instead of appropriate waste disposal facilities, sewage was collected in an underground vat, and the contents seeped onto the hapless workmen maintaining the underground railway. There were problems in the club itself, too, as the toilets regularly overflowed. By 1965, Liverpool Council had ordered McFall to make repairs, and as he had spent his money on a recording studio, he didn't have the resources.

Perhaps the Beatles could help out? When they were in Atlanta in August 1965, George Harrison told a reporter, "We've done our bit for the club, and I don't think we owe it anything else."

In February 1966, fans barricaded themselves in the Cavern overnight to keep out the bailiffs. There was an appeal for funds, and a revamped Cavern, under new management, was opened in June 1966 by Harold Wilson—an early example of a prime minister seeking the teenage vote.

The club ran into further problems when British Rail wanted to expand its underground network. A ventilation shaft was needed, and the ideal location was the Cavern. In March 1973, the bulldozers moved in, and the Cavern was buried in rubble. Once the network was completed, the Cavern's site became a parking lot. The new Cavern reopened in a basement across the street, and this site subsequently found fame under a different name as the punk club Eric's.

Following John Lennon's death, there were plans to develop a combination of offices, shops, a pub, and a club. Five thousand of the Cavern's original bricks, with plaques, were sold for charity, each costing £5. At a Beatles auction today, a single brick will fetch £300. The old Cavern has been not only re-created but also expanded with a second stage and, most significantly, a fire exit. Paul McCartney played at the Cavern in December 1999 to promote his album *Run Devil Run*; the show was broadcast on the BBC and over the internet.

Today it is possible to visit the Cavern either as a tourist attraction in the daytime or for a show in the evening. Both '60s bands and contemporary music are featured. Many key names play the Cavern, and it is still a magical place to see anyone.

Merseyside Jazz Union

Cavern Club

MEMBERSHIP CARD
1960 SEASON

Ending 31st December, 1960

THE Cavern CLUB

MEMBERSHIP
1962 SE

Ending 31st

THE Cavern CLUB

MEMBERSHIP CARD
1962 SEASON

Ending 31st December, 1962

Opposite, left: The most unlikely management for a beat club: Bob Wooler (left) with Ray McFall outside the Cavern, 1964.
Opposite, right: Bob Wooler's calling card as "Dee Jay Compere" at the Cavern. He also had a card calling himself a rock 'n' roll consultant.
Above: The Beatles at the Cavern, August 1962. Ringo, out of shot, had just joined the group.
Left: Various membership cards for the Cavern. Membership had to be renewed annually.

4 THE BIGGEST BAND ON MERSEYSIDE

"John Lennon described us as the old buggers who didn't want the Beatles on stage, which was correct. We lived in different worlds."

JOHN LAWRENCE, MERSEYSIPPI JAZZ BAND

Left: One of several photographs from Harry Whatmough's session with the Beatles in March 1962. Epstein wanted a promotional card for the Beatles in their new Beno Dorm suits. The cards were given away at dances and a female fan might tear off the photo of her favorite Beatle and pin it to her top.

THE BEATLES' ROUSING PERFORMANCE AT Litherland Town Hall in December 1960 had given them immense confidence. They were pleased with their temporary bass player, Chas Newby, and although he was offered a permanent role, he preferred to continue with his studies. Stu Sutcliffe visited Liverpool with Astrid and made a few guest appearances, but mostly the group had reduced itself to a four-piece band, with Paul McCartney playing bass.

The clubs in the Liverpool suburbs were now featuring rock 'n' roll, and a central venue was needed. The Cavern's new owner, Ray McFall, had the Blue Genes (later the Swinging Blue Jeans)—who played a cheerful mix of trad, music hall, and skiffle—host guest nights, and as a result, the Beatles made their evening debut at the Cavern on March 21, 1961. The Beatle fans got there early and took up the front row seats, watching the Blue Genes with disdain.

McFall remembered the occasion well. "Afterwards, the Blue Genes tackled me in Mathew Street, and they were most upset. As far as they were concerned, the Beatles didn't have the musical talent, and they weren't clean, fresh, and well-organized. I said that if the place is full, there are a lot more people watching the Blue Genes."

And he was right. The Beatles were becoming a local sensation, often playing three gigs in a day—the Cavern at lunchtime and two clubs in the evening. Then they were gone again. From the end of March to early July 1961, they played at the Top Ten in Hamburg. When they returned (this time with leather jackets *and* leather trousers), they were even better.

But there was tension between the jazz bands and the beat groups. Although the members of the Merseysippi Jazz Band were only in their thirties, John Lennon would refer to them as "the old buggers." Geoff Davies was, at the time, one of the jazz fans: "The first night I saw the Beatles was at an all-night session with Kenny Ball and various jazz bands. About one o'clock in the morning, there was a break and we heard a rock band tuning up. It was a horrendous noise; it was loud guitars and drums and screaming. We got a pass to leave and went to

Top: The Beatles in front of the Commer van in Mathew Street. Ray called it the "Cavernmobeel."

Above: The Swinging Blue Jeans after their success with "Hippy Hippy Shake." (Left to right) Ralph Ellis (a John Lennon lookalike), Les Braid, Norman Kuhlke, and Ray Ennis.

Below and right: The Beatles at St. John's Hall in Bootle on Friday, January 6, 1961, when they appeared with the Searchers for the promoter Dave Forshaw. The Beatles were paid £6.10s for the show (the Searchers were paid £4) and, based on the Beatles' performance, a £7.10s payment was arranged for their next two performances.

the Pier Head for a pie and a cup of tea. We came back, and Kenny Ball came on and he was great."

LOCAL PROMOTION

On July 5, 1961, with a sponsorship of £50, Bill Harry launched a fortnightly newspaper, *Mersey Beat*, based on the Liverpool rock 'n' roll scene. The name he chose gave a name to the music. His only full-time employee was his girlfriend and later wife, Virginia, but articles were contributed by both John Lennon (as Beatcomber, a pun on the "Beachcomber" author who wrote a long-running surreal column, "By the Way," in the *Daily Express*) and Bob Wooler.

There were high-quality photographs, even if published on newsprint, from Dick Matthews, Peter Kaye, Graham Spencer, and Mike McCartney.

The innovative publication could be bought at news agents, clubs, and record shops, and each issue regularly sold five thousand copies. Brian Epstein was impressed to find such a thriving music scene on his doorstep, and he wrote reviews for *Mersey Beat*, mostly of show albums, which naturally were available at NEMS. *Mersey Beat* created a real pride among the bands, who loved being featured in their own newspaper. At the time, the local newspaper, *Liverpool Echo*, carried only small ads for the venues and very little else.

Even the Beatles could be booked for the wrong event. On Sunday afternoon, October 15, 1961, the Beatles were part of a very curious lineup on a variety show for charity at the Albany Cinema, Maghull. The organizer, Jim Gretty, whose main job was to sell guitars for Frank Hessy, had secured the local comedian Ken Dodd to top the bill, followed by a lineup that covered country and western, Gilbert and Sullivan operettas, opera and comedy acts, as well as the Beatles. Ken Dodd recalls, "I got there about 3 p.m., and there was chaos. People were walking out because some idiots on stage were making the most terrible row. I said to the producer, 'You've got to get these fellers off, they're killing the show.' They got them off, and while I was changing, one of these idiots came in and said, 'Somebody told me that if we gave you our card, you might be able to get us a few bookings.' I threw the card away. Later on, when I worked with the Beatles, Paul McCartney said, 'We've worked with you before, Doddy.' I replied, 'No, you've never worked with me, lad.' He said, 'Yes, we have, at the Albany, Maghull.' I asked him, 'That noise wasn't you, was it?' and he said, 'Yeah, we were rubbish, weren't we?' to which I replied, 'You certainly were. I had you thrown off.'" Jim Gretty knew Brian Epstein, so history might have been very different indeed if Jim had given Brian a couple of tickets for that show.

Four days after they had been thrown off the stage, the Beatles teamed up at Litherland Town Hall with Gerry and the Pacemakers for a single performance as the Beatmakers. "We were just waiting to go on, and someone said, 'Why don't we go on together and have a laugh?'" says Gerry. "Paul, John, and then me all played the piano. Les Maguire, our pianist, played saxophone on 'I'm Walkin'.' We had two drummers and two drum-kits, and it was great, a spontaneous one-off thing that you couldn't repeat."

THE SIGNING

Polydor Records had issued a single in Germany, "My Bonnie" by Tony Sheridan, accompanied by the Beatles (as the Beat Brothers). The Beatles had given a copy to Bob Wooler to play during changeovers at the Cavern and elsewhere. Keen Beatles' fans wanted to buy it, and one of them, Raymond Jones, went into NEMS. Brian Epstein didn't know of the single but promised to order it.

Above: The program for the variety show at the Albany cinema in Maghull, to raise funds for a new ambulance.
Center: The Beatles' first single "My Bonnie," backing lead singer Tony Sheridan as the Beat Brothers. This was the second issue of the German single released in January 1962.
Opposite, top right: Handbill for the Beatles' season at Aintree Institute in 1961. The Beatles kept up these weekly appearances for Brian Kelly until the end of September.
Opposite, below: Mr Brian Epstein.

Raymond Jones, who now lives in Spain, recalls, "Everybody else was listening to Lonnie Donegan and Cliff Richard, and then I heard the Beatles and I thought, 'This is it. They are doing the songs I love, and they are so fantastic at it.' I loved them, and I followed them around—Hambleton Hall, Aintree Institute, Knotty Ash Village Hall, and, of course, the Cavern. I asked Brian Epstein for the record, and he said, 'Who are they?' I replied, 'They're the most fantastic group you will ever hear.' That's it. End of story." In a way, yes, but Raymond Jones's request set a chain of events in motion that meant popular culture would never be the same again.

Being conscientious, Epstein wanted to track down the single and thought it best to ask the Beatles themselves. He had noticed them in the shop and seen their photographs in

Jive Fans This Is It!

MEET THE BEATLES
every Saturday at
AINTREE INSTITUTE
(BUSES 20, 21, 22, 30, 61, 91, 92, 93, 95, 96 & 500 TO BLACK BULL, NEXT DOOR)

YES ! PAUL, JOHN, GEORGE AND PETE
will be playing for you exclusively at Aintree Institute,
every Saturday, starting 12th August 1961.
You must be there, too !
Come early and bring your friends !
Jiving from 7-30 to 11 p.m.　　　　　　　Admission 4/-
Aintree Institute Your Saturday Dance Date

Polydor

35

M 45

24 673 A

GEMA
BIEM

N H

My Bonnie
Twist
(trad. / Sheridan / Berlie)
Tony Sheridan
& the Beat Brothers

Mersey Beat. Bill Harry arranged for him and his assistant, Alistair Taylor, to visit the Cavern for a lunchtime session on Thursday, November 9, 1961, and they saw the Beatles' last five songs. "We looked out of place in our grey suits and white shirts," said Alistair Taylor. "We didn't particularly care for beat music, but we were totally converted. Afterwards, we went to lunch at a nearby restaurant, Peacock's, and Brian said, 'Shall we manage them?' He knew they were something special. I know I was impressed by them singing one of their own songs, 'Hello Little Girl.'"

That evening the Beatles played the Litherland Town Hall for what would be the last time. The two Brians, Epstein and Kelly, were not friends, as Kelly, something of a cheapskate, objected to Epstein raising the Beatles' fee. When the Beatles appeared at Aintree Institute on January 27, 1962, Kelly paid him in loose change. Epstein recalled in his autobiography,

THE FAMOUS Tower BALLROOM
—ACCOMMODATING 3000 DANCERS...

"I kicked up an awful fuss, not because £15 isn't £15 in any currency, but because I thought it was disrespectful of the Beatles."

The following day, November 10, 1961, the Beatles played the first of Sam Leach's "Operation Big Beat" evenings at the Tower Ballroom, New Brighton. These dances proved very successful, with audiences building up to five thousand. That first night the Beatles played two sets and in between played at the Knotty Ash Village Hall. After their second set, they had a foolhardy car chase through the Mersey Tunnel with Rory Storm and the Hurricanes that nearly ended in disaster.

Top, left: Poster for the first "Operation Big Beat"—a series of concerts at the Tower Ballroom, New Brighton.
Top: The Tower Ballroom was the Beatles' biggest venue to date. Epstein had his doubts as it could be rough: he once saw a table fly through the air when he was having a quiet drink at the bar.
Center and below: Operation Big Beat tickets. Note the transportation arrangements: relatively few fans would have had their own cars.

THE TOWER

THE TOWER BALLROOM AT NEW BRIGHTON, WALLASEY, was one of the largest venues on Merseyside, and it played a significant role in the history of the early Merseybeat sound.

Construction of the Tower began in 1896 and was completed in 1900. This glorious and elegant Victorian steel structure resembled the Eiffel Tower in Paris and stood just over 567 feet high. At the time it was the tallest structure in Britain. The tower had four lifts, and from the top visitors could see areas of the Lake District, the Welsh mountains, and the Isle of Man. Beneath the tower stood the theater and opulent ballroom. One of the largest in the world, the ballroom had a stage, a sprung dance floor, and the capacity to hold five thousand people. The Tower was surrounded by approximately thirty-five acres of land, a part of which formed the Tower Gardens, with lakes, fountains, pools, and pathways to explore the grounds.

During the First World War, the Tower's steel structure fell into decay. Due to the high cost of renovation, it was dismantled in 1919–21. The theater and ballroom remained, and during World War II its basement was used as an air-raid shelter.

In the '60s, the Tower Ballroom hosted a series of historical performances. "Operation Big Beat" was the brainchild of local promoter Sam Leach. The first "Operation Big Beat" event was held at the Tower Ballroom on November 10, 1961. The lineup for this six-hour extravaganza featured the Beatles (who performed two sets), Rory Storm and the Hurricanes, Gerry and the Pacemakers, the Remo Four, Kingsize Taylor and the Dominoes, amongst others. With approximately three thousand people attending the event, the venue's capacity ensured local groups an exposure to thousands of fans at one gig, which the smaller venues on Merseyside could not provide.

"Operation Big Beat II" was held two weeks later, on November 24. Building on their initial success, Sam Leach introduced the "Big Beat Sessions," which took place every Friday. On December 1, 1961 the Beatles appeared with Rory Storm and the Hurricanes, Dale Roberts and the Jaywalkers, Derry and the Seniors, Kingsize Taylor and the Dominoes, and Steve Day and the Drifters. The following week, the Beatles supported Davy Jones (not to be confused with the Davy Jones who found rock 'n' roll fame with the TV Monkees) with Danny Williams, Rory Storm and the Hurricanes, Gerry and the Pacemakers, Earl Preston and the Tempest Tornadoes

Above: The magnificent Victorian Tower at New Brighton. When it was completed in 1900 it was the tallest structure in Britain. The Ballroom underneath was one of the largest dancehalls in the world.

and the Remo Four. Ever the businessman, Brian Epstein saw an opportunity to position the Beatles as stars in their own right by booking them alongside established musicians performing at the Tower, such as Bruce Channel and Delbert McClinton in June 1962, Joe Brown and his Bruvvers in July 1962, and Little Richard in October 1962.

The Beatles performed numerous times at this venue from November 10, 1961, to July 14, 1963, when they played their last performance alongside Gerry and the Pacemakers.

Sadly, the building, which played a central role in the golden era of Merseybeat, no longer exists: the building and surrounding areas deteriorated through neglect, and in 1969 it was destroyed by fire.

THE WORD GETS AROUND

All the beat groups on Merseyside took a close interest in what their competitors were doing. They would take songs from each other, and nearly every group was performing "What'd I Say," "Some Other Guy," and "Roll Over Beethoven." The musicians would move from one band to another, so the main topic for both fans and musicians would be the growing network of groups and venues. The Litherland Town Hall gig in 1960 had created a stir, and with the Beatles' regular appearances throughout '61 and '62, combined with Epstein's management, the group began to generate an increasingly loyal, local fan base among youngsters and fellow musicians.

"The Beatles went to Germany, and then there was a buzz going round, 'Have you heard the Beatles?' and I pooh-poohed it. We played Lathom Hall, and the Beatles were on, and I had my arms folded on the dance floor, thinking, 'Let's see how good you are,' and they started off with 'Lucille,' and they were so tight and so good that every hair on my neck stood up. It was a completely new sound, and I had never heard anything like it. I know now that they had the drums mic'd up, they had a mic in the bass drum, so I know what the secret was."

PETER COOK, THE TOP SPOTS

"I dated Paul McCartney on and off, as everybody dated everyone in Liverpool—there was nothing in it—and one night he said to me, 'Do you want to hear the song we've written?' and he sang the first verse of 'Please Please Me' with all those 'Come ons.' I burst out laughing and said, 'That's not a song, don't be silly.' I was also dating Frank Ifield, and I told him about the Beatles and sang 'Please Please Me' to him, and he said, 'Well, I don't have to worry about that.'"

IRIS CALDWELL, RORY STORM'S SISTER

Above, left: Paul followed by fans in Liverpool. Even in the Beatles' heyday, Paul would walk or take public transport.
Opposite, clockwise from top left: The Beatles had a fan club long before they had a hit record and this special night for their fans was arranged just before they went to Hamburg to open the Star-Club. Everyone who attended the event was given a fan club photograph with a printed message on the reverse. The fans had them personally signed by the Beatles.

THE BEATLES FAN CLUB
PRESENTS

"BEATLES FOR THEIR FANS"

AN EVENING WITH GEORGE, JOHN, PAUL & PETE

GUEST ARTISTES WILL INCLUDE

THE FOUR JAYS

AND THE BEATLES' FAVOURITE COMPERE

BOB WOOLER

7-30 p.m., THURSDAY, APRIL 5th, 1962

AT THE CAVERN

TICKETS 6/6d.

Ticket holders will receive a FREE PHOTOGRAPH and may apply for
FREE Membership of the Fan Club. (See over).

With love to Beryl from George Harrison
xxxxxxxxx
love to Beryl
from John Lennon

With Best Wishes
from

love to Beryl
from
John

Paul McCartney
xxx

Pete

George

Love to Beryl
from
Pete Best
xxx

THE BEATLES

April 5th 1962

"Prior to the Beatles going to Hamburg, they were just another band, but now they had a totally different drive, much tighter guitar licks, and a format that really worked."

JOE FAGIN, THE STRANGERS

"On the evening session [February 23, 1962] at the Cavern, people were queuing just after midnight for the show the next day. George Harrison came in his Ford Anglia and asked them how long they had been waiting. He knew that they would be out in the elements all night, and he went to the Pier Head and brought back twenty-five steak-and-kidney pies."

JOEY SHIELDS, BLUES SINGER

Within two months of Brian Epstein's decision to manage the Beatles, he secured the band an audition at Decca Records—on New Year's Day, 1962. With their road manager, Neil Aspinall, it took the Beatles ten hours to reach London in a snowstorm. The Beatles recorded fifteen songs, including three of their own compositions, in quick succession, but—perhaps because of the grueling journey—they were below par.

Decca's A&R man, Mike Smith, had to audition another band, the smart and professional Brian Poole and the Tremeloes from Barking, Essex. Smith reported back to his boss, Dick Rowe, and they chose Poole's group, which made many hit records. On any other day that would have been a decent decision, but on this day they had turned down the Beatles—a stigma that would follow Rowe and Smith for the rest of their lives.

Back home, *Mersey Beat* conducted its own poll to find out who were Liverpool's most popular acts. The Beatles topped the list in January 1962, followed by Gerry and the Pacemakers,

Above: NEMS on Great Charlotte Street, Liverpool. Brian Epstein's office was at the other NEMS store, just around the corner on Whitechapel. The first NEMS record store in Liverpool city center was opened in December 1957 by matronly singing star Anne Shelton. Brian ran the record division and his brother Clive sold the electrical goods.

Johnny Sandon and the Remo Four, and Rory Storm and the Hurricanes.

On February 23, 1962, the Beatles played an evening show at the Cavern with the Searchers and then branched out into Southport, with regular bookings at the Kingsway Casino and a Rock 'n' Trad Spectacular at the Floral Hall. The Beatles returned to Hamburg in April 1962 for the opening of the Star-Club; while there, they heard of an audition for EMI's Parlophone label.

On June 6, 1962, the Beatles (John, Paul, George, and drummer Pete Best) came to the EMI studios at Abbey Road. Producer George Martin looked in partway through the

On October 27, the Beatles gave their first recorded interview, broadcast on the Cleaver and Clatterbridge hospital radio on the Wirral peninsula. Monty Lister was the interviewer but his guests, Peter Smethurst and Malcolm Treadgill (with the microphone), both seen here with the Beatles, asked additional questions. The interview contained this telling section:

MONTY LISTER: Then there's George Harrison.
GEORGE: How do you do.
MONTY: How do you do. What's your job?
GEORGE: Lead guitar and sort of singing.
MONTY: By playing lead guitar does that mean that you're sort of leader of the group or are you . . . ?
GEORGE: No, no. Just . . . well you see, the other guitar's the rhythm. Ching, ching, ching, you see.
PAUL: He's solo guitar, you see. John is in fact the leader of the group.

audition as Ron Richards, his assistant, was recording them for a potential single, sound engineered by Norman Smith. From that day forth until 1965, Norman was to work on all the Beatles' recordings at EMI.

The Beatles played a stage favorite, "Besame Mucho" (taken from the Coasters' repertoire), and three songs written by John and Paul: "Love Me Do," "P.S. I Love You," and "Ask Me Why." Pete's wayward drumming on "Love Me Do" sealed his fate.

"I thought Pete Best was an essential part of the Beatles because of his image," explains George Martin. "There was a moody James Dean look about him. But I didn't like his drumming. I didn't think it held the band together as it should have done, and I was determined that the Beatles weren't going to suffer because of it. I told Brian that I was going to use a session drummer when we made the records. I didn't realize that the other boys had been thinking of getting rid of Pete and that my decision was the last straw that broke the camel's back.

So Pete was given the boot, poor chap, thereby missing out on a vast fortune. It was hard luck on him, but it was inevitable."

In August 1962, Pete Best, according to the Beatles' wishes, was sacked by Brian Epstein and replaced by Ringo Starr. Johnnie Hamp filmed their gig at the Cavern on August 22 for Granada TV, and after "Some Other Guy" the audience can be heard calling "We want Pete." Tomatoes were thrown at the Beatles—as the Cavern was adjacent to fruit and vegetable warehouses, the punters could pick up rotten fruit on the way in. It is often said that some angry fan gave George a black eye, but this was really because a jealous boyfriend didn't like the way his girl was looking at George.

After rerecording "Love Me Do," the single was released on Friday October 5, 1962, and the Beatles celebrated by signing copies in NEMS and other local stores. Brian Epstein took the release of "Love Me Do" as his opportunity to position and firmly establish the band. The Beatles had only played

Above: The Empire Theatre on Lime Street was part of the Moss Empires chain and many rock 'n' roll stars played here, including Gene Vincent and Eddie Cochran in 1960. The Quarrymen appeared in talent shows here in 1957 and 1959, and the Beatles' first appearance at the Empire was with Little Richard in October 1962. George played here with Delaney and Bonnie on the first night of a tour in 1969.

the Liverpool Empire at talent contests as the Quarrymen. The American rock 'n' roll star Little Richard had just finished a UK tour (the Beatles had played at Little Richard's performance at the Tower Ballroom, New Brighton, on October 12), and Epstein added an additional booking for October 28, at Liverpool Empire, supported by UK chartmakers Craig Douglas and Kenny Lynch. This was Epstein's opportunity to showcase the Beatles as potential stars.

Craig Douglas, who had topped the UK charts with "Only Sixteen," recalls, "The Beatles had been hired as my backing group, and although they couldn't read music, we bashed through the songs for a couple of hours at rehearsal, and they did a very good job. They finished their performance with 'Love Me Do,' which brought the place down, and I had to follow that, which was very difficult but great fun. After the show I went back to Chester (where I was staying), and I had to go through the Mersey Tunnel. I gave the guy in the tollbooth a £5 note, but he didn't have any change. I went back to the Empire and the first person I saw was John Lennon. I said, 'Can you change a fiver?' and he said, 'Change one? I've never even seen one.' He lent me a half-crown so I could go through the tunnel. I never gave it back to him. I'd forgotten about it until now."

On December 15, 1962, the Beatles took part in the *Mersey Beat* poll awards show from the Majestic Ballroom, Birkenhead. They won, and Lee Curtis and the All-Stars (with Pete Best) came in second.

Billy J. Kramer remembers it well: "The Beatles did 'Please Please Me,' and I told George Harrison that they should record it. It was the first time I'd heard them perform an original number. Brian Epstein said in his book *A Cellarful of Noise* that the first time he heard the Beatles he knew that they were going to be as big as Elvis. Well, the first time I saw them at Litherland Town Hall I thought that, and when I heard them play 'Please Please Me,' I knew it."

The Beatles finished the year with two weeks at the Star-Club. They were reluctant to return to Hamburg, as things were happening in the UK. They had a chart single with "Love Me Do," and they had recorded their next release, "Please Please Me." Brian Epstein placed a full-page ad in *Mersey Beat* headed "1962—The Beatles' Year of Achievement."

So the year ended with the Beatles playing in a seedy area of Hamburg. Their one single, "Love Me Do," had made number 17, which was a start, and nothing would be the same again. Although they made several appearances in Liverpool in 1963, their attention was very definitely elsewhere.

Left and above: Poster and program for the Beatles' October 28, 1962, performance at the Liverpool Empire (when they were low down on the bill). This was the band's first appearance at a major provincial theater. Brian Epstein was taking no chances by having Little Richard topping the bill. The Georgia Peach (his own name for himself) had left rock 'n' roll to become a minister but now he was back, screaming his head off.

"Pete Best left the group by mutual agreement. There were no arguments or difficulties, and this has been an entirely amicable decision."

Press comment from the Beatles, *Mersey Beat*, August 23, 1962

LOVE, LOVE ME DO

John Lennon had been playing the harmonica for some time (he had stolen one from a shop on the first trip to Hamburg), but the inspiration for its use in "Love Me Do" was the Top 10 single "Hey! Baby," by the American singer Bruce Channel, with harmonica solos by Delbert McClinton.

In June 1962, Channel and McClinton were on a UK tour, and they played the Tower Ballroom, New Brighton, with the Beatles as one of the supporting acts. Bruce Channel says, "There were lots of kids there, a whole sea of people, and I said to Delbert, 'They can't all have come to see us.' We soon found out that the Beatles were very popular in the area.

"John Lennon was interested in Delbert's harmonica sound, so Delbert played something for him. Evidently John kept the idea and used it for the sound on 'Love Me Do.'" You might expect Bruce to have been annoyed by that, but no: "It's a thrill to know that our record influenced the Beatles, that our music was appreciated by a group of that stature."

George Martin had some reservations about the commerciality of Lennon and McCartney's songwriting and wanted the Beatles to record a new song, "How Do You Do It?" written by Denmark Street writer Mitch Murray. "How Do You Do It?" was a cheeky pop sing-along, ideal for Bobby Vee or Adam Faith, but the Beatles preferred material with a harder edge. The Beatles returned to Merseyside, and their second visit to Abbey Road was on September 4, 1962. By this time Ringo Starr, who had left Rory Storm and the Hurricanes, was the group's new drummer, and they recorded "Love Me Do" and "How Do You Do It?"

Just one week after that session, the Beatles were back at EMI, rerecording "Love Me Do" as well as "P.S. I Love You" and an

Left: The Beatles listening carefully to George Martin in their early days at Abbey Road.

Above: The white label copy of "Love Me Do" (reproduced here at actual size) sent to disc jockeys in 1962. The spelling of McCartney's name was corrected on the pressing for the public. Epstein was furious, saying that the disc jockeys would give out wrong information. He was also disappointed with the music publisher, Ardmore and Beechwood, and switched to Dick James for the next single.

TOWER BALLMOOM · NEW BRIGHTON
Wooler SHOW
NUMBER ONE ... STAR SHOW LICENSED BARS

THE BEATLES
Parlophone Recording Artistes

HEY! BABY
BRUCE Channel
AND DELBERT McLINTON (HARMONICA)
DIRECT from AMERICA! with THE BARONS

THE BIG THREE
THE Statesmen the NORTH'S FABULOUS FIVE!
THE FOUR JAYS

THURSDAY 21ST JUNE · 1962 7·30 TO 12 P.M.

TICKETS IN ADVANCE 5'6 ON THE NIGHT
AVAILABLE FROM NEMS · RUSHWORTHS · LEWIS'S HE STROTHERS Etc. & TOWER BALL

early version of "Please Please Me" performed like a Roy Orbison ballad. George Martin recognized the potential of "Please Please Me" but wanted a faster arrangement and stronger harmonies. Being unsure of Ringo Starr on the September 4 recording, he brought in session drummer Andy White, reducing Ringo Starr to tambourine for "Love Me Do" and maracas for "P.S. I Love You." White, who sometimes played with the Vic Lewis Orchestra, was married to Lyn Cornell, a singer with another Liverpool act, the Vernons Girls.

Aside from denting Ringo's confidence, Andy White's drumming made little difference to the sound. The two versions of "Love Me Do" are similar: you can spot the difference by listening for the tambourine. Their first single paired the September 4 take of "Love Me Do" and "P.S. I Love You," but that take was replaced

Top: John showing the harmonica—a key sound on "Love Me Do" and "Please Please Me."
Above: Bob Wooler had a stash of these posters. Every year he would sell one at the Liverpool Beatles Auction, for around £1,300. Note the misspelling of McClinton and the inclusion of the Four Jays who became the Fourmost.
Opposite: The demo record sleeve (top) that contained the white label copy of "Love Me Do," which was sent to disc jockeys. Here, however, it is shown with the red label "Love Me Do" single. Also shown (bottom) is the sleeve and record of "Love Me Do" issued for general release.

by the Andy White version on re-pressings. White's version made the *Please Please Me* LP. Both versions were included on the twelve-inch commemorative single issued in 1982.

Yankel Feather, who owned the Feathers club in Liverpool city center, was one of the first to hear the single. "One day I came into my club early, and I was surprised to see that Brian Epstein was the first customer. He was very happy, as he had come back from London with the first pressings of the Beatles' single, 'Love Me Do.' Well, after listening to people like Sacha Distel, who was making jazz records you could dance to, and the soprano Adèle Leigh, this was a shock to my system. It sounded like an Arab dirge. I said that they would never get anywhere with that, and he looked disconcerted. I don't think he ever forgave me."

George Martin, too, was unsure about the single. "I had reluctantly agreed to release 'Love Me Do' as the first single. I thought it was the best of the bunch and John's harmonica was very appealing. It got to number 17, and I never thought it would do much better, because I didn't think the song had much to offer." The single went on to top the American charts in 1964, and the B-side, "P.S. I Love You" also made the U.S. Top 10. "Love Me Do" reached number 4 in the UK on reissue in 1982.

"The first time I had heard them perform 'Love Me Do,' I thought it sounded more skiffley than rock 'n' roll," comments Ray Ennis of the Blue Genes. "I know that EMI had wanted Paul to play a string bass on it, because Paul had asked Les Braid how to do it, because there are no frets on a string bass. Les showed him how to get the octave with his left hand. The Beatles did try it with a double bass, but they preferred it with the electric."

On its release, NEMS published its own Top 10 in the windows of its shops, and "Love Me Do" was naturally number one. However, rumors spread that Brian Epstein had bought ten thousand copies of the single and thereby ensured its chart rankings. His fellow impresario, Joe Flannery, claimed to have seen the copies, but Tony Barrow, who became the Beatles' press officer, does not believe the story. "I know for a fact that the record sold enormous quantities on Merseyside as soon as it was released. I was writing the Disker column for the *Liverpool Echo*, and either my wife or I would ring the various wholesalers in the city to find out what had been selling. This wasn't ringing NEMS, but the wholesalers, to find out what retailers were ordering. As far as the wholesalers were concerned, 'Love Me Do' was the number one best-selling record, and that had nothing to do with Brian Epstein directly buying, or not buying, a quantity of records.

"All those who were involved with the Beatles, including the Beatles themselves, got a greater thrill out of seeing 'Love Me Do' creep into the charts and make number 17 than all the records that went to number one. Later on it was a foregone conclusion that the records would go straight to the top, so the nail-biting, white-knuckle ride as far as the Beatles were concerned has to be the very first single, 'Love Me Do.'"

BRIAN EPSTEIN

Roy Plomley: "Were you born in Liverpool?"
Brian Epstein: "Yes, I'd say it was essential."

DESERT ISLAND DISCS, BBC, 1964

JUST OUTSIDE LIVERPOOL FOOTBALL CLUB'S GROUND AT Anfield stands Epstein's Guest House, which caters to both Beatle and soccer fans. It was the home of Brian Epstein's grandparents, and Brian spent the first months of his life there.

Brian Samuel Epstein, the first child of Harry and Malka (known as Queenie), was born in a private hospital at 4 Rodney Street, Liverpool, on September 19, 1934. Harry managed a furniture store, and he and Queenie moved to 157 Queens Drive, a large house in Wavertree, given to them as a wedding gift. A second son, Clive, was born in 1937.

When he was ten, Brian was expelled from Liverpool College for drawing obscene pictures, and he had a troubled adolescence, moving from one school to another. He left Wrekin College at fifteen with no qualifications but a desire to be a dress designer. His father told him not to be ridiculous; instead, he became a promising furniture salesman in the family business.

During his year of National Service in 1952, Brian was discharged for impersonating an officer. He then took to studying acting at the Royal Academy of Dramatic Art, but this was cut short after his arrest for importuning men outside a public restroom, and he returned to the family business. He maintained a lifelong love of the theater: he once saw a play starring Vivien Leigh four times in one week.

In 1957, Harry Epstein opened NEMS (North End Music Stores) in Whitechapel in the city center, and Brian showed his adeptness in organizing the record department. They would stock every record that was issued in the UK, and he created a foolproof system for reordering.

He took the lease on a flat in Falkner Street, largely for his male companions. Although homosexuality was illegal in Britain at the time, there were gay pubs—the Lisbon, Bar Royal, and the Magic

Above: It wasn't only the Beatles who won awards. Brian Epstein was voted Britain's best dressed man. He was also regarded as one of the UK's most eligible bachelors.

Clock (known as the Magic Cock)—that he frequented. His passion for rough trade created trouble. After Epstein picked up a man in a toilet, he became the victim of blackmail, and the man was jailed. When the blackmailer came out of prison, Epstein took him for lunch.

"It's sometimes said that he signed the Beatles because he was in love with John," comments Alistair Taylor. "But I know for a fact that he signed the Beatles because he thought they were incredible. For a time, he was still doing his day job selling records at NEMS, and sometimes he would tell me not to tell his father that he had gone to London to deal with the Beatles. Harry guessed where he was, but he was more worried than annoyed."

Brian Epstein first saw the Beatles in November 1961 and offered to manage them at a meeting at NEMS on December 3, 1961. The Beatles signed the contract on January 24, 1962, and it is said that Brian didn't sign because his word was his bond. However, we do not have all the copies of the contract and he might have left his own copy unsigned. The contract was redrawn a couple of times, but in 1963 Epstein was taking 25 percent of their earnings, which was less than many managers of the day: Colonel Parker took 50 percent off Elvis Presley. Epstein was also acting as the Beatles' agent for no additional fee. He changed the group's stage image—smartening them up, no smoking and no clowning around—which clearly worked. Once, when the Beatles were recording, he made a suggestion, only to be rebutted by John, who said, "You stick to your percentages, Brian, we'll look after the music."

"Brian Epstein was a helluva nice guy," says '50s hitmaker Craig Douglas. "He didn't look like an agent or a manager of a beat group. I'm not sure that the music was really his bag, but he was a very intelligent man, and he knew his business. He was very nice, very articulate, and very smartly dressed."

Following the recording of "Love Me Do," comments from Brian to his associates and friends, such as Yankel Feather and his brother Clive, illustrate his belief that the Beatles were going to be legendary, but if that was the case, why did he bother to sign up so many other performers? Ray Coleman, then with *Melody Maker* and later

Above: Ray McFall's Cavern diary for November 1961—illustrating how far the Cavern had moved away from its origins as a traditional jazz club. The Beatles and Gerry and the Pacemakers alternated lunchtime sessions for almost the entire month. Brian Epstein saw the Beatles here for the first time on Thursday lunchtime, November 9, 1961.

Above: Key figures in the NEMS roster in 1963: four Beatles, Gerry and three Pacemakers, Billy J Kramer in the middle of four Dakotas, and Brian Epstein.

BILLY J.KRAMER
recording for the Parlophone label

THE FOURMOST
recording for the Parlophone label

Epstein's biographer, hit on the answer: "Brian Epstein saw something chemical about them that was even bigger than the music. He became hooked on the minefield of talent in Liverpool, and he enjoyed their company. It was so much more than just another job to him. He already had money and, unlike a married man, he didn't have other priorities. Although his homosexuality is important in understanding him, the crucial factor is that he was available for work twenty-four hours a day. He made the Beatles very famous very quickly, and if there were mistakes later on, it was usually the fault of others."

It would have been impractical for Brian and the Beatles to have remained in Liverpool. The music industry was centered in London, the national newspapers were in Fleet Street, and the bulk of radio and TV programs were made there. Epstein relocated in October 1963 to offices next door to the London Palladium in central London. Some of the staff did not want to move, and their fan club secretary, Freda Kelly, remained in Liverpool. "It was very spontaneous," says Tony Bramwell, who at the time assisted Neil Aspinall as a roadie. "He said he was moving to London, and were we coming?"

From 1963–65 the Beatles' hectic schedule of touring, filming, and television interviews did not impede Epstein's management of other successful acts: Cilla Black, Gerry and the Pacemakers, Billy J. Kramer, the Big Three, and the Fourmost. He thought Tommy Quickly and Michael Haslam had the ability to become big stars, but it didn't happen. By having so many acts on his books, he could, like Larry Parnes, create his own touring packages for the UK. He leased the Saville Theatre in London in 1965 to promote plays by new writers, and in 1966 he introduced rock 'n' roll performances to the theater's program.

Above, above right, and below: Billy J. Kramer, the Fourmost, and the Big Three. With their blend of comedy and rock 'n' roll, the Fourmost deserved more success, although they had Top 10 singles with "Hello Little Girl" and "A Little Loving."

In that same year, the Beatles stopped touring, and Epstein had no intention of following the group into transcendental meditation. While they were in Bangor with the Maharishi, he died at his London address over the August bank holiday weekend of 1967. The coroner ruled that he had taken "incautious self-overdoses" of sleeping tablets. Many considered Epstein's death a suicide because the Beatles had outgrown him and were no longer touring. However, he was still running the Saville Theatre in London and was planning to make Cilla Black a major movie star. Also, the Beatles wanted him to renegotiate their EMI record contracts, as the Rolling Stones were earning more from records than they were. Epstein is buried in the Jewish cemetery at Long Lane in Liverpool; his parents and his brother Clive are buried close by.

The world's most famous rock managers are Colonel Parker, Brian Epstein, and Allen Klein. Parker treated Elvis like a cash cow, signing him for appalling movies and turning down less lucrative but more worthy offers (such as the movie of *West Side Story*). Klein was a rogue who bullied his way to secure top rates for his clients (and himself). Unlike either of these managers, Epstein genuinely cared for his clients and never did anything underhanded. So many groups of the '60s were ripped off; even though the Beatles did not have the best deals, they were fairly treated and never had to worry about receiving their money. As a result, they could concentrate on being creative.

Epstein has been criticized for being out of his depth, but this is unfair. No group had ever been as big as the Beatles, and he was in uncharted waters. His major error was in negotiating the merchandising rights (a practice that was then in its infancy). In America, he all but gave away the rights for Beatles merchandise, as the manufacturers had to pay Epstein only 10 percent of the profit.

Epstein's good points far outweighed his bad, and it was unjust that he did not receive an MBE along with the four Beatles in 1965. Still, their designation was a vote-catching move by Prime Minister Wilson, and perhaps he saw no advantage in honoring the manager as well.

Johnny Rogan, author of a book on rock managers, *Starmakers and Svengalis*, says, "Brian Epstein was an excellent manager, and he's only been criticized from the money aspect—he should have made more money from the Beatles. He had integrity, as he didn't get involved with tax avoidance schemes, although there was some trouble with *Help!* There are so many different functions

Top: Gerry and the Pacemakers with new recruits.
Above: Pattie Boyd, George Harrison, and Brian Epstein are toasting Cilla Black on reaching No.1 in Britain with "Anyone Who Had A Heart," 1964. The song was originally written by Burt Bacharach and Hal David for Dionne Warwick.

that a manager has to perform, and many of the qualities are mutually exclusive—some pamper their artists and others treat them like frightened schoolchildren. Being a good manager is about getting success for your artist to accord with your personality and theirs, and that's what he did."

5 THE LEAVING OF LIVERPOOL

"From late on in 1963, the Beatles weren't really a Liverpool group. They had become a metropolitan group, although they often mined their Liverpool past for their records. The thing about the Beatles is that they made changes. They made so many changes, and that is what is exciting about them."

JON SAVAGE, WRITER AND MUSIC HISTORIAN

Left: From June 1962 to April 1963, the Beatles played the Majestic Ballroom, Birkenhead, seventeen times. The Ballroom was owned by Top Rank, and the Beatles played at many more of their venues across the UK. Pictured here is their final appearance at the Majestic on April 10, 1963.

THE BEATLES' GROWING POPULARITY AND DEMANDING schedule led to a decline in their regular performances in Liverpool. In the first half of 1963 the group had three nationwide tours, and on the occasions that they did return to the city, their appearances caused an overwhelming reaction from their growing local fan base. In January 1963, the Beatles played the infamous Grafton Rooms in West Derby—infamous because the dance hall became known for its "Grab a Granny" nights. Although Billy Kinsley was playing with the Merseybeats at the Cavern, he recalls returning home and witnessing a surprising sight. "It was 11.30 p.m. There were hundreds of fans waiting for buses in West Derby Road, singing 'Please Please Me.' Everybody was happy, and there was no trouble. It was an incredible atmosphere, and I knew something special had been happening."

The following month, the Beatles were off on a nationwide tour with Helen Shapiro, who had shot to stardom as a fourteen-year-old schoolgirl in 1961. During a break in the tour, they completed the songs for their first album, *Please Please Me*. The Helen Shapiro tour didn't come to Merseyside but during breaks in the schedule they performed at the Cavern, February 3 and 4; the Locarno (next door to

Above: The Beatles at the Assembly Hall in Mold, Flintshire, on January 24, 1963. A plaque outside the building commemorates this performance. Earlier in the day, the group had appeared at NEMS to sign copies of their single "Please Please Me."
Top left and left: Poster for the Grafton—a hundred tickets for this dance were stolen but as they were numbered, the hapless fans who bought them were told they were invalid. Handbill for the Locarno—the free gift for the first 500 ladies was a photograph of the Beatles.

the Grafton), February 14; Queen's Hall, Widnes, February 18; the Cavern, February 19; and the Majestic Ballroom, Birkenhead, February 21.

At the Cavern performance on February 19, the Beatles played with Lee Curtis and the All Stars, the Pathfinders, and Freddie Starr and the Midnighters. Just as the Beatles went on stage, Pete Best, who at that time was playing with the All Stars, would have heard Bob Wooler read out a telegram sent care of the Cavern Club. It was from Brian Epstein, and it confirmed that "Please Please Me" had climbed to the top of the *New Musical Express* chart. Rather than cheering, the audience went silent: they sensed that the Beatles no longer belonged to them. Even in early 1963, there was something unique about the Beatles. Although Gerry and the Pacemakers, the Searchers, and Billy J. Kramer all had hits that went to number one, there was not the same feeling of loss among the city's teenagers.

The telegram sent to the Cavern Club was all showmanship. The Beatles already knew they were number one. Earlier that day, photographs of the group were taken by Michael Ward in Brian Epstein's office and alongside Liverpool landmarks (Pier Head, Water Street, Derby Square); at that time only one of these was published.

After the short break, the Helen Shapiro tour continued, but the nearest it came to Liverpool was the Odeon in Southport on March 1. The tour finished on March 3, and the following night,

the Beatles played the Plaza Ballroom, St. Helens. This gig marked the first time they received a £100 fee. Geoff Taggart of the Zephyrs was there: "I was outside the Plaza, and I was talking to Billy J. Kramer when Brian Epstein came across to me and asked me what I thought of 'the boys,' which was how he described the Beatles. I said, 'They're all right, but this chap is better.'"

Within a week of finishing the Helen Shapiro tour, "the boys" were back on the road as part of a touring package with the American stars Chris Montez and Tommy Roe. Their only date in Liverpool throughout this tour was at the Empire on March 24, two days after the release of *Please Please Me*. The tour ended with a performance at De Montfort Hall, Leicester, on March 31. Throughout April and the first few weeks of May, the Beatles played individual dates, but the only ones around Merseyside were their last appearance at the Majestic Ballroom, Birkenhead, on April 10; an all-nighter at the Cavern, April 12; the Mersey View Pleasure Grounds at Frodsham, April 20; and the Floral Hall, Southport, on April 23.

Above, left: The Beatles at the Cavern on February 19, 1963. They shared the bill with Lee Curtis and the All-Stars. It was the last time they would come into contact with Pete Best.
Above, right: The Beatles' first nationwide tour was with Helen Shapiro in February 1963. Here's John with Helen on TV's *Ready, Steady Go!* in October 1963.

Ron Ellis, a librarian and part-time impresario, saw them at their Floral Hall appearance in Southport. "I used to import records from America, and I would sell them to groups like the Beatles. John Lennon gave me a list of titles that he wanted from the States, and Ringo added some more. Later on, I cut up the list into one-inch squares, and I sold them to schoolgirls who came into the library where I worked, for 10d each. I thought this was fantastic at the time, but of course, I'd have made a lot more if I'd kept it in one piece." This anecdote also reveals that, at this point, the Beatles had no immediate plans to visit America themselves.

Although the Beatles had not yet performed in the States, their tours in the first half of the year had secured a growing national following in Britain. Much closer to home, the vast number of venues on Merseyside, plus the dedicated and specialist *Mersey Beat* newspaper, had, over the previous two years, interested and attracted the Manchester bands to the Liverpool music scene, and they came to the city whenever they could. In '63, Brian Epstein, who managed Billy J. Kramer, teamed Billy with the Dakotas, a Manchester group, and the Hollies were even billed as Manchester's answer to the Beatles. "I didn't sense that intercity rivalry between Manchester and Liverpool too much, and I certainly had nothing to do with it myself," comments Graham Nash of the Hollies. "I always thought that there was a lot of great talent in both cities, which should really go without saying."

The Beatles were still seen on occasion at a late-night haunt, the Blue Angel. Mike Evans of the Clayton Squares recalls,

Top: The Beatles first wore their famous collarless suits on the Helen Shapiro tour. Made by Dougie Millings, a tailor based in Soho, London, each suit cost £31.
Center: The Beatles' final appearance at the Majestic Ballroom.
Left: The Blue Angel, a late night haunt for beat groups in the early '60s.
Opposite, top: The Beatles backstage at the Roy Orbison tour with Gerry and the Pacemakers.
Opposite, left: Flyer for the Chris Montez and Tommy Roe tour. Gordon Mills of the Viscounts befriended Brian Epstein and they would frequent gambling clubs together.
Far right: Although the Beatles hadn't won anything, in view of their recent success they were added to the bill at the *NME*'s Poll-Winners' Concert, and performed four songs.

"I was in the Blue Angel one night in 1963. The Beatles had been spending a lot of time in London, and George Harrison said to me, 'I've heard this great group, they do all the old Muddy Waters and Chuck Berry songs, and they're almost as good as the Roadrunners [a local R&B group].'" Mike asked him who they were, and George replied, "The Rolling Stones."

During the Beatles' three nationwide tours in the first half of 1963, the group was part of the lineup that opened for the headline act. Throughout the tours, fans would scream for the Beatles, often overpowering the act that had top billing—a phenomenon previously unseen.

On May 18, the Beatles began their nationwide tour with the American star Roy Orbison, playing the Liverpool Empire on May 26. Roy had been booked as top of the bill (replacing Duane Eddy), but after a couple of shows he accepted second billing to the Beatles. He had a remarkable ability to control the crowd and wasn't fazed by the audience's screaming for the Liverpudlians. He told his band to play the first song pianissimo. This was a brilliant move, as the audience had to stop screaming in order to hear him. The tour finished on June 9, and the Beatles had a short break, next appearing at the Grafton Rooms on June 12.

On June 18, 1963, Paul McCartney celebrated his twenty-first birthday with a party at Auntie Gin's house in Huyton. John had just returned from a trip to Spain with Brian Epstein—a curious move, as most husbands would have returned to their wife and child after touring—but possibly John wanted to assert his leadership of the group over Paul McCartney. As John and Bob Wooler

BEATLEMANIA HITS LIVERPOOL... AND THE UK

By the end of 1963, you could buy Beatles caps and Beatles capes, Beatles wigs and Beatles hankies, Beatles boots and Beatles suits. In one day, Sayers, a chain of Merseyside bakery shops, sold twenty-five thousand guitar-shaped cakes incorporating a photograph of the Beatles. Whenever they returned to their home city, the band caused a sensation.

"Originally the Beatles fan club was at my home address. I must have been stupid to do that, as the post office van would roll up at four o'clock every day with two sacks of mail for me. My dad was looking through the sacks to find his telephone bill or rate demand or letter from his sister. He even went to see Brian Epstein to complain, and I nearly lost my job over it."

FREDA KELLY, BEATLES FAN CLUB SECRETARY

"On the last night at the Cavern, the crowds outside were going mad. By the time John Lennon had got through the cordon of girls, his mohair jacket had lost a sleeve. I grabbed it to stop a girl getting away with a souvenir. John stitched it back on. They may have altered their style elsewhere, but they didn't do it at the Cavern. They were the same old Beatles, with John saying, 'Okay, tatty-head, we're going to play a number for you.' There was never anything elaborate about his introductions."

PADDY DELANEY, DOORMAN AT THE CAVERN

Right: Crowds gathered before every concert, waiting for the arrival of the Fabs.
Opposite, far left: Opening the sacks of fan mail that arrived every day.
Opposite, left: Although the Beatles were rarely seen in jeans, Brian Epstein approved of this advert with a local manufacturer. Lybro soon switched allegiance to the conveniently named Swinging Blue Jeans.

"The reaction was incredible. I didn't think at the time that it was going to be their last night at the Cavern, but now I look back on it, it's obvious. The Cavern could never have afforded them again."

BOB McGRAE, CAVERN EMPLOYEE

"John Lennon said to me, 'For God's sake, Alistair, we're only a pop group.'"

ALISTAIR TAYLOR, BRIAN EPSTEIN'S ASSISTANT

Following a contract signed with the Grafton Rooms in January, the Beatles were obliged to play at the venue on August 2, 1963. "Brian Epstein couldn't pull them out of that appearance, and he was furious, as he had other things in mind," explained Bob Wooler. "He was calling the promoter all sorts of names, but he didn't use four-letter words, as he never did that."

The contract contained a clause that prevented the Beatles' appearing in Liverpool in the weeks before, but not after, that appearance, so Brian asked Bob Wooler to take the Beatles for the Cavern on the following night. "I resented this, as he was only doing it to get at the promoter, Les Ackerley, and anyway, I had the groups booked in. If I'd said no, he would have gone to Ray McFall, who would have said, 'Of course we'll take them.'" The Beatles were paid £300, and Brian restricted the audience to five hundred. "I can't blame Brian, as he had seen how crowded the Cavern became, and he had to think of the Beatles' safety," explains Bob. "The admission price was ten shillings, so we only collected £250 on the door. All the staff had to be paid, and the other groups too, so we made no profit that night."

Because a full evening's entertainment had already been booked, the show ran from 6 p.m. to 11.30 p.m. "It was more Mercenary Beat than Mersey Beat that night," recalled Bob. "The Escorts and the Merseybeats still wanted to be paid; the kudos of being on with the Beatles wasn't enough. We all felt it was their swan song, and we would never have them at the Cavern again. Brian Epstein still owes the Cavern six dates for the Beatles, as he kept pulling them out of bookings by saying, 'You wouldn't stand in the boys' way, would you, Bob?'"

The Merseybeats, with lead singer Tony Crane, performed on the night of "Mercenary Beat." "It surprised us that the Beatles had decided to come back for a show at the Cavern. We had just recorded 'It's Love That Really Counts.' We were on just before the Beatles and so were delighted with our reception, as everybody was cheering. The Beatles had long faces, and John Lennon was saying, 'We never should have come back here.' Everything was sweaty, and once the walls got wet, the condensation came down onto the stage and it was dangerous.

were walking to the marquee, Bob asked, "How was the honeymoon, John?" John, who had been drinking, hit Bob and knocked him out. Billy Hatton of the Fourmost and then Billy J. Kramer rescued Bob from further punishment, and Lennon snarled, "You're nothing, Kramer; we're the top." Bob Wooler was taken to the hospital, and the fight, through Allan Williams's intervention, made the *Daily Mirror*.

This was the first piece of bad publicity received by a Beatle, and Epstein successfully limited the potential damage. Bob received £200 in damages and an apology from John Lennon, though clearly it was written by Epstein. In 1972, John Lennon commented that he was committed to peace following the incident. "That really is nonsense," said Bob Wooler. "I would hate to think that I was the catalyst for 'Imagine,' because I detest the song."

Throughout the summer, the Beatles were playing single-appearance gigs, usually at British seaside resorts—Great Yarmouth, Blackpool, and Rhyl—with weeks in Margate, Weston-super-Mare, Llandudno, and Bournemouth. The MC was often the comedian Jack Douglas, who appeared in the British *Carry On* movies. His slapstick-style of humor depended on simulated body spasms.

Opposite: Paul signing a fan's magazine at NEMS. **Far left:** The Merseybeats at the Cavern in 1963. **Left:** Copying the Beatles' lead, one of the younger bands, the Escorts, in 1964.

It fused the electrics and the lights went out. Normally, John Lennon would have cracked jokes while somebody fixed it, but he was in such a bad mood that he came off stage."

The Beatles were hampered by a loss of power and light, but they gave a memorable performance. In front of the stage, girls invariably filled the seats. A brave lad managed to sit in the front row, and when the girls frowned at him, he offered them his knees and remained seated. At the end of the evening one girl asked how his knees were. He said, "What knees?"

At the end of August 1963, the Beatles played a week at the Odeon Cinema in Southport. During this week, they filmed a live performance one morning at the Little Theatre, Southport, for a very good and now historic BBC documentary, *The Mersey Sound*, directed by Don Howarth. It also featured the Undertakers and Group One, and the locations included NEMS and Ringo's family home in the Dingle.

The Beatles' independent performances throughout August and the first two weeks of September were then followed by a mini tour of Scotland at the beginning of October. On October 13, they starred in *Sunday Night at the London Palladium*. Their appearance on the TV show exposed the group to a television audience of approximately fifteen million—over one in four of the UK population. The hysteria of the Palladium's audience propelled the group into a media spotlight that was to follow them throughout their career, and the phrase "Beatlemania" was coined by the *Daily Mirror*. At the end of October the Beatles returned from a five-day tour in Sweden. They were

greeted at London Airport by approximately ten thousand screaming fans.

On November 1, 1963, the Beatles began their fourth tour—and their first British tour as top billing—which continued throughout November and December. On November 4, they appeared in the Royal Variety Show at the Prince of Wales Theatre. By this point Beatlemania had spread across

Above: The Beatles on TV's *Sunday Night at the London Palladium*, October 13, 1963.

the country, and although the bill included nineteen acts, the Beatles stole the show: the whole country loved the audaciousness and wit of John Lennon's remark "Would the people in the cheaper seats, clap your hands. And the rest of you, if you'll just rattle your jewelry." Jack Douglas couldn't have topped that.

Epstein's schedule was demanding, but even by Beatles' standards, they had a hectic day on Saturday December 7. "We recorded *Juke Box Jury* at the Liverpool Empire," says host and DJ David Jacobs. "I spoke to the audience first, and as you can imagine, they were very excited, and I knew that if I wasn't able to control them, they would run riot. When I introduced each of the Beatles on stage, the cheering was so great that it sounded like the entire jet fleet of British Airways taking off. Once they'd settled down, the boys were tremendous, and it was a great program. It was broadcast that evening, and we had our highest-ever viewing figure; something like twenty-four million people watched it that night."

Following the recording of *Juke Box Jury*, and in front of a 2,500-strong audience that included their Northern Area fan club members, the group performed a special concert at the Empire. The concert was aired later that evening on BBC-TV as part of a program called *It's the Beatles!* In the evening, the Beatles moved to the adjacent Odeon Cinema for two performances of their autumn tour with the Brook Brothers, the Kestrels, and, from Liverpool, the Vernons Girls.

The Beatles continued with their British tour, and the last 1963 performance in Liverpool was on December 22 at the Liverpool Empire for a preview of their Christmas show, an uneasy mix of beat music and pantomime. The show then moved to Finsbury Park, London, for its run from December 24, 1963 to January 11, 1964. The audiences, naturally, couldn't stay quiet for the sketches. Ten thousand people queued for tickets at the Liverpool Empire—a 2,500-seat venue—and an angry chief constable said that the cost of the policing (£350) should be the Empire's responsibility.

Throughout 1963, the Beatles' fan base had grown steadily. The display and scale of hysteria was unprecedented and Alun Owen was to draw on the phenomenon of Beatlemania as part

Top: Poised for their bow at the end of the Royal Command Performance, November 4, 1963, and (above) meeting the Queen Mother afterwards.
Opposite, top left: George and the boys during the taping of an edition of *Juke Box Jury* at the Liverpool Empire, part of the Northern Area Fan Club Convention on Saturday December 7, 1963.
Opposite, below: Inside of the program showing the day's running order.
Opposite far right, top: Delighted girls with their Beatles tickets.
Far right, below: The Beatles refuel at a canteen late in 1963. Ringo flicks through a copy of the British satirical magazine *Private Eye*, first published in 1961.

MISS

THERN AREA FAN CLUB CONVENTION
IRE THEATRE, LIVERPOOL : SATURDAY 7th DECEMBER 1963

Doors Open 1.30 pm for 2.00 pm

* Programme of Events *

FAN CLUB CONVENTION EDITION OF BBC TELEVISION'S

★1 JUKE BOX JURY

PANEL MEMBERS: JOHN LENNON, PAUL McCARTNEY, GEORGE HARRISON, RINGO STARR.

SECOND JURY: ANNE COLLINGHAM AND BETTINA ROSE (JOINT NATIONAL SECRETARIES OF THE OFFICIAL BEATLES FAN CLUB) FREDA KELLY (MERSEYSIDE AND LANCASHIRE AREA SECRETARY OF THE FAN CLUB).

* Interval *

Special *Fan Club* stage performance by

★2 THE BEATLES

to be filmed by BBC TELEVISION who will
screen the programme under the title
"IT'S THE BEATLES!" this evening

of the comically self-referential plot in the Beatles' film *A Hard Day's Night* (1964). Henceforth the Beatles were to change and influence popular culture, not just in their music but also in fashion, attitudes, lifestyle, merchandise, and marketing. The Beatles had had an extraordinary year in 1963, but it was to be outclassed by 1964.

⑥ A HARD DAY'S NIGHT

"I had thought that the Beatles would simply turn up at the Town Hall and that would be that. I had not anticipated that thousands would turn out in the streets to see them."

ERIC HEFFER, LIVERPOOL WALTON MP, 1964–1991

Left: The Beatles with Wilfrid Brambell on the set of *A Hard Day's Night*.

352 BEA/1/2(ii)

54. Avondale Rd.
Liverpool 15.

2-2-1964.

My dear Lord Mayor,

For some time now, I, no doubt like every other citizen in Liverpool, have followed the career of the "Beatles" with particular interest.

Their rise to the height in the entertainment world has been phenomenal, until today they are great international artists.

They are in their own way, wonderful ambassadors for our city. Their conduct has been of the highest order, and we can be justly proud of them. Their appearance at a Royal Command performance, their successful visit to Paris, and their forthcoming trip to the United States. are all achievement which have helped to put Liverpool on the map.

I am therefore suggesting that we as a city should do something to honour them, and I would propose that consideration be given to a civic reception in their honour.

I hope that my suggestion will meet with your full approval and support.

Yours sincerely,
Eric S. Heffer.
(City Councillor.)

4th February, 1964.

Dear Mr. Epstein,

As you may well imagine, I have been following the activities of "The Beatles" with tremendous interest during the last few months, particularly since their brilliant performance on the occasion of the Royal Command Show. The Lady Mayoress and I would like to have an opportunity of receiving and entertaining them at the Town Hall but, knowing how full their programme has been during recent months, I feel quite sure that this would not have been possible. I sincerely trust that their visit to the United States will be a great success and perhaps on their return to their native city we could arrange a mutually convenient date for a civic reception.

I wonder if you would be good enough to bear this in mind and perhaps in due course you could kindly let me know, at least provisionally, of a suitable date when I might invite them here.

Yours sincerely,

Lord Mayor.

B. Epstein, Esq.,
NEMS Enterprises Ltd.,
24, Moorfields,
LIVERPOOL.

Left: Eric Heffer, the legendary Merseyside MP who dedicated his life to the working people. When he suggested honoring the Beatles with a civic reception at the Town Hall, he was a city councilor; however in the Labour General Election victory of 1964, he was elected MP for Liverpool Walton. He died in 1991.

Main inset: Some of the correspondence that led to the Beatles' civic reception at Liverpool Town Hall on July 10, 1964, beginning with (left) Eric Heffer to the mayor of Liverpool; the mayor's consequent correspondence to Brian Epstein (center); and Epstein's speedy reply to the mayor, informing of the imminent first visit to America, and the impending production of the first Beatles' movie, *A Hard Day's Night*. Note Brian Epstein's "Yours respectfully." He knew the etiquette for writing to a lord mayor.

ONE OF THE LUCKIEST MEN IN LIVERPOOL WAS A *Liverpool Echo* newspaper reporter named George Harrison. He milked the fact that he had the same name as a Beatle, and he traveled around the globe with them, reporting back for the paper. He described what a nice bunch of lads they were, and very soon the *Liverpool Echo* was promoting teenage culture in a big way.

In February 1964, the lord mayor of Liverpool, Alderman John McMillan, prompted by Eric Heffer (a city councillor at the time), wrote to Brian Epstein and invited the Beatles to a civic reception at the Town Hall. Brian Epstein explained that the Beatles were on a tight schedule and would be making a feature film. He commented, "the boys and I set forth for the United States tomorrow morning." The Beatles were number one in America with "I Want to Hold Your Hand," but he could

NEMS ENTERPRISES LTD
DIRECTORS: B. AND C.J. EPSTEIN

24 MOORFIELDS, LIVERPOOL, 2   TELEPHONE CENtral 0793

Reference BE/MTD

6th February, 1964.

My Lord Mayor,

Thank you very much for your charming letter of the 4th
instant. As you probably know the boys and I set forth
for the United States tomorrow morning. On their return the
boys have an intense filming schedule, which will take them
up to the end of April. They will then be resting during
most of the month of May. So therefore whilst I look forward
very much to accepting your very kind invitation, for which the
boys and I am most appreciative, I think the actual date will
have to be left in abeyance for the present.

With many thanks and best wishes.

Yours respectfully,
BRIAN EPSTEIN

Alderman John McMillan,
Lord Mayor,
The Town Hall,
LIVERPOOL.

OFFERS CONTAINED IN THIS LETTER DO NOT CONSTITUTE CONTRACTS
LICENSED ANNUALLY BY THE LIVERPOOL CORPORATION

not have imagined how ecstatic their reception in America
would be. Epstein wrote that he would consider the lord
mayor's request on his return.

Following performances in Versailles and Paris, the Beatles
went to America for *The Ed Sullivan Show* and had concerts
at the Washington Coliseum and Carnegie Hall. At one point

Top right: Epstein's "boys" disembark to a tumultuous reception at John F.
Kennedy Airport on February 7, 1964. Around 4,000 fans and over 200
press photographers greeted their arrival at New York's international airport.
Formerly known as Idlewild, the airport had recently been renamed in honor
of the fallen president, assassinated barely three months before.
Center right: Further unprecedented scenes greeted them in New York City.
Bottom right: Their historic appearance on *The Ed Sullivan Show*,
8 p.m., Sunday, February 9, 1964, watched by a record TV audience of 73
million coast to coast—around 38 percent of the entire American population.
Even crime was said to have stopped during their ten-minute appearance.

in April 1964, the Beatles held the top five places on the U.S. charts with "Can't Buy Me Love," "Twist and Shout," "She Loves You," "I Want To Hold Your Hand," and "Please Please Me." In June they toured outside the UK, performing in Denmark, Netherlands, and Hong Kong, and they spent a fortnight in Australia and New Zealand. The group took civic greetings to Liverpool, Australia.

Impresarios, like politicians, seek publicity, and Brian Epstein quickly realized how a civic reception could be turned to the Beatles' advantage. It could be combined with the northern premiere of their first film, *A Hard Day's Night*. Despite the impression, the film was not shot in Liverpool, but it was written by Alun Owen, a Welshman based in Liverpool who had previously written the highly acclaimed TV drama *No Trams to Lime Street*.

Although the script appears spontaneous and neatly captures the Beatles' personalities, it was carefully crafted by Alun Owen, who had spent some time with the group in October 1963. He was working concurrently on Lionel Bart's Liverpool musical, *Maggie May*.

Top, left: Film director Dick Lester with the Beatles on the set of *A Hard Day's Night.*
Top, right: Filming *A Hard Day's Night.*
Opposite: The Beatles arrive at Speke Airport for their triumphant homecoming. Ringo waves to the crowd and talks to Alderman David Cowley, who in 1965 became Liverpool's youngest lord mayor.

The film was directed by Richard Lester, who had previously worked with the Goons, and although he planned to shoot it in Liverpool, the Beatles' overwhelming popularity made this impossible. Instead, the film was made at Twickenham Studios and Marylebone Station (when it was closed) as well as a few London locations.

The Beatles returned to Liverpool on July 10, 1964, for a reception at the Town Hall and the northern premiere at the Odeon cinema. This was a master stroke by Epstein. "It was the icing on the cake, the perfect double whammy," says press officer Tony Barrow.

A few days before the event, the MP Charles Curran criticized John Lennon's book, *In His Own Write*, and thought it made an admirable case for raising the school leaving age. John's sister Julia says, "The bad English in the book was deliberate. John loved Lewis Carroll. Mr. Curran was under the misapprehension that John had been a poor boy at a downtown secondary modern school. Nothing could have been further from the truth." John naturally found this funny, and the incident demonstrates how even the critics played into the Beatles' hands.

THE HOMECOMING

The official film premiere was held at the London Pavilion on July 6, four days before the northern premiere; the event stopped traffic in the West End. Nevertheless, the Beatles were apprehensive about making an ostentatious return to Liverpool. Beatlemania was reaching new heights, and they feared that their friends, and the Cavernites, might not care for the attention the band was receiving. David Jacobs flew with them and reveals, "They were very worried, particularly George, that there wouldn't be anybody at the airport to meet them. When we were coming in to land, I looked out of the porthole, and I saw below me a sea of what looked like currants. There were more people to meet them than they had ever had before. They were worried that Liverpool wouldn't want to turn out for their own boys. How wrong could they be?"

The Beatles gave a press conference at Speke Airport and were interviewed by Gerald Harrison for BBC-TV: "All four could speak at any time, and they had this reputation of being the scourge of interviewers. John, in particular, was devilish.

Technology was in its infancy as far as video recording was concerned, and we had a live outside broadcast camera in Liverpool that was being relayed to Manchester, where there was a cumbersome recording machine, an Ampex. It was so rudimentary that I had to give a voice cue over the air and say 'stand by, Ampex,' which sounded very important. The four Beatles were sitting opposite me and John leaned across and said, 'hello, Ampex' and carried on a surreal, imagined conversation with the machine. That flustered me, as we had not even started the interview, and there he was taking over the engineering facilities in Manchester."

The weather was good, and the cavalcade was cheered all the way to the Town Hall. Over 150,000 lined the streets. Six hundred guests had been invited to the reception. The Quarrymen, Pete Best, and Allan Williams were not invited,

and even Bill Harry had to lobby hard for a ticket. "Previous members of the band, no. Previous managers, certainly not," says Tony Barrow.

The only other beat group to be invited was the Chants, a black act whom the Beatles had accompanied on occasion. They were championed by the MP, Bessie Braddock. Eddie Amoo says, "We were really there because Bessie Braddock had us under her wing. There wouldn't have been a chance in hell of five black boys going in a cavalcade through Liverpool to the Town Hall otherwise."

By then the lord mayor of Liverpool was Louis Caplan, a long-standing councillor who campaigned for the underprivileged. He had one unusual quality for a politician: nobody said a bad word about him. As he was unmarried, his sister, Fanny Bodeker, was appointed Lady Mayoress. When the Beatles came onto the balcony, she waved to the crowds as though she were the fifth Beatle.

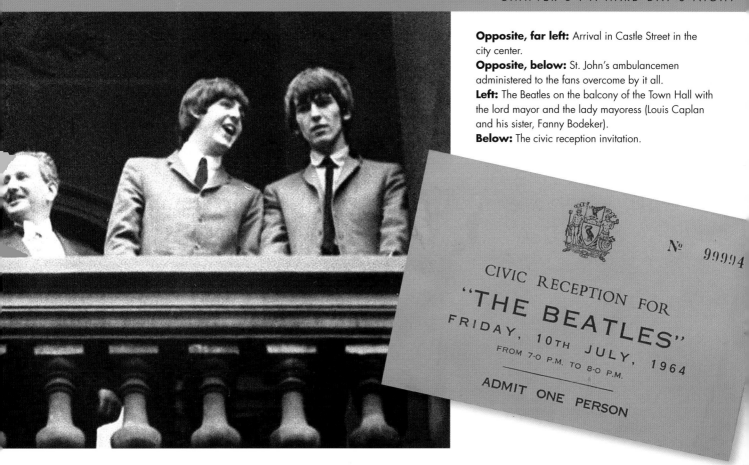

Opposite, far left: Arrival in Castle Street in the city center.
Opposite, below: St. John's ambulancemen administered to the fans overcome by it all.
Left: The Beatles on the balcony of the Town Hall with the lord mayor and the lady mayoress (Louis Caplan and his sister, Fanny Bodeker).
Below: The civic reception invitation.

Nº 99994

CIVIC RECEPTION FOR
"THE BEATLES"
FRIDAY, 10TH JULY, 1964
FROM 7-0 P.M. TO 8-0 P.M.

ADMIT ONE PERSON

There is a revealing moment in the film footage in which John can't resist a Nazi salute, and Ringo cautions him. "It shows the way that John Lennon behaved in general. He was not a balanced figure," says solicitor Rex Makin. "Maybe he had touches of genius in his own field, but his behavior and his life were bizarre."

"I know for certain that the Beatles didn't expect the streets to be so full," says Freda Kelly, Beatles Fan Club secretary. "I was behind them when they walked onto the balcony, and I could see that Castle Street was just a mass of people. The lads were laughing, and everyone was smiling. It was a really happy occasion, and the whole atmosphere was lovely."

"I would estimate that 60 percent of the crowd was hysterical young girls, and when the Beatles appeared on the balcony, they went ballistic," remembers Terry Baldwin, who was on duty with the St. John's Ambulance Brigade. "We didn't have oxygen, and they were

hyperventilating. The flimsy metal barriers were just pushed to one side. The authorities had wanted to maintain a huge space in front of the Town Hall, but the crowd just surged forward. Even the police horses were hemmed in. The Beatles could see what was happening, and they were told by the police to leave the balcony.

"We were overwhelmed, as we had nowhere to put the casualties. The crowd was not giving way, and we were hemmed in. Young girls were passed over heads to us. The police did a sterling job but had to send for reinforcements. We were unable to get our vehicle out, so it was a static first aid post. Early on we had our stretchers laid out in line, but they were just trampled on. It was chaos, but fortunately nobody was seriously hurt."

Liverpool's overwhelming response to the Beatles' return inspired and captured the imagination of the young, up-and-coming Liverpool bands. Frankie Connor of the Hideaways recalls, "We had been rehearsing that afternoon,

BEING THERE

The Beatles' Liverpool performances in '63 generated fan frenzy, but the Northern premiere of *A Hard Day's Night* on July 10, 1964, was to top all previous reactions from their home town. The following day, the *Liverpool Echo* reported on the event with the headline, "The Night of 100,000 Screams."

"I was standing on the corner of Canning Street and Catherine Street as they drove past. They had come from the airport, and now they were approaching the city center. I was waving like everybody else. I was with my girlfriend, who was a big Cavern Beatles fan, and when they saw her, they gave her a very deliberate, personal wave. It was so odd, as I had seen them around Liverpool only just over a year earlier as part of the scenery. It all happened so quickly."

MIKE EVANS

"I can understand the fans thinking that the Beatles had deserted them. I know the feeling, and you can't please everybody, but it was an amazing day. I saw the footage not so long ago in a museum in New York, and it really hit home to me how remarkable the Beatles were."

BILLY J. KRAMER

Above: Willy Russell, young Caverndweller and author of *Educating Rita*, *Shirley Valentine*, and *Blood Brothers*.
Opposite: The crush outside the Town Hall as the Beatles arrive.

"I'll always remember the incredible sight of seeing the Beatles come out onto the balcony of the Town Hall. It is still something of a romantic place for me whenever I pass it."

WILLY RUSSELL

"I could never understand why some Liverpool people were against the Beatles. We had local talent that was conquering the world and bringing pride to the city. You'd have to be full of sour grapes to attack that. They were the same people who attacked the Beatles for getting MBEs."

BILL HARRY, EDITOR, *MERSEY BEAT*

"The whole council was there, and by Jove, that was a lot of people! We were all chatting with the Beatles in the Town Hall, and they were unaffected and were still only boys, of course. They didn't mind talking to lord mayors and bishops at all, and they came across as very natural, very pleasant young men. The council too was very gracious in the way it dealt with them, and little did we know that they would become the most famous Liverpudlians of all time."

VINCENT BURKE, LIVERPOOL COUNCILLOR

"The city fathers met the Beatles, and the more important the person was, the more careful the Beatles had to be. They couldn't offend lord mayors and senators. It's a pity that the people who had firsthand contact with the Beatles were often the most undeserving people."

TONY BARROW, BEATLES' PRESS OFFICER

"I was fortunate, as my father was a member of Liverpool City Council, and he had an invite for the reception. Every councillor got two tickets, and my father didn't want to see those 'long-haired yobbos,' but my mum liked the Beatles a bit and so she took me. The lord mayor lived near us, and when he saw me, he said to John Lennon, 'Here's a young customer for you,' and John Lennon leaned over and said, 'Hello, young customer,' and shook my hand."

MARC GAIER

"The only time the Tuxedos got top billing at the Cavern was when the Beatles came to Liverpool for the premiere of *A Hard Day's Night*. The whole of Liverpool was lining the streets, but none of them came to the Cavern. We got about eighty people, and I wouldn't be surprised if that booking wasn't one of Bob Wooler's jokes."

BILLY BUTLER, THE TUXEDOS

"When we were all settled down in the cinema with our chocolates, John came on stage with the curtains still closed behind him, and he said, 'Where's my family?' and we shouted, 'We're here, John, we're here.'"

JULIA BAIRD, JOHN LENNON'S HALF-SISTER

and we went round to the Town Hall. The streets were full of people, and we saw the boys on the balcony. We thought, 'That could be us: we could be the next Beatles,' but every Liverpool group thought like that."

Despite his creation of Albert Steptoe (the lead character in the BBC-TV comedy series *Steptoe and Son*), Wilfrid Brambell, who played Paul's mischievous grandfather in *A Hard Day's Night*, was ignored at the reception and later wrote disparagingly about his hard day's slight: he was a theatrical personality, and the Beatles were of a lower order. David Jacobs says, "I didn't mind being second fiddle or even fifth fiddle to the Beatles. I was surprised that anybody should be offended. It was their day, and it was wonderful to be part of it."

The Beatles took a car to the Odeon cinema for *A Hard Day's Night*, again with cheering fans all along the route. Beatle fan Jean Catharell recalls: "My brother said that he had good news and bad news. The good news was that he had got me a ticket, but the bad news was that I would have to go on my own. I didn't mind that. The street was crowded, and the police were forcing everybody back from the doors. Pushing my way through the crowd, a policeman stopped me, and I said I had a ticket sewn inside my jacket because I was terrified of losing it. Throughout the film people were screaming. I didn't see much of it, as for most of the film I sat with my back to the screen looking up to where the Beatles were sitting. I went back three days later with my friend to see the film to find out what it was about."

After the event, John met up with Pete Shotton and they went to Mendips to reminisce. The Beatles returned to the road for a few UK dates and a trip to Stockholm; then from August 19 on they toured America, returning to start their only UK tour in 1964 on October 9. On the eve of the 1964 general election (October 15), Brian Epstein sent Harold Wilson—the leader of the Labour party and MP for Huyton—a telegram: "Hope your group is as much a success as mine." Labour was elected with a slim majority, and Eric Heffer, who had initiated the Civic Reception, became an MP.

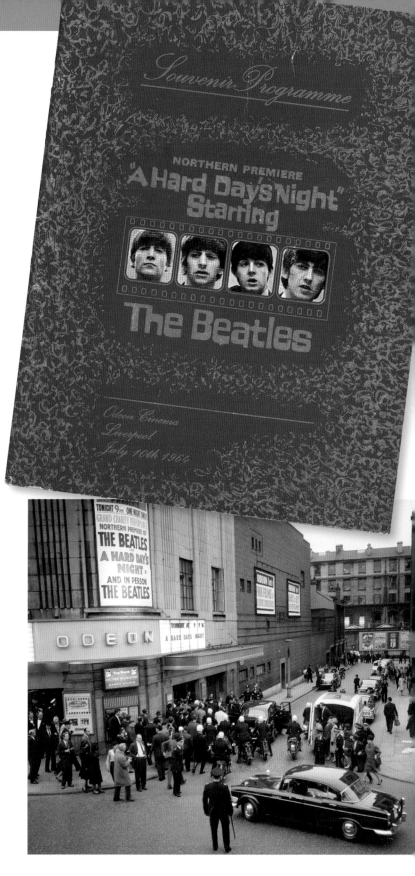

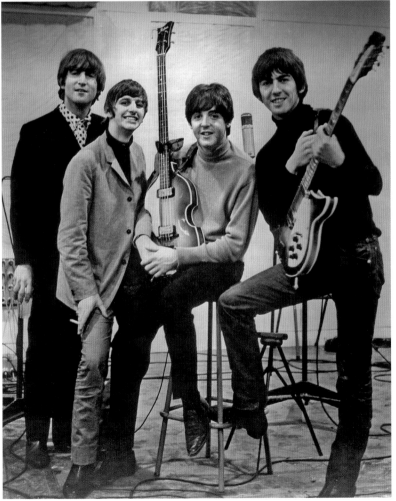

The Beatles toured the UK with Motown star Mary Wells, Tommy Quickly, and the Remo Four in October and November. They appeared at the ABC Cinema, Wigan, and at the Liverpool Empire, where Tommy's performance was recorded for a live single. Colin Manley of the Remo Four recalled, "We went on with Tommy Quickly for a short spot just before the Beatles. John Lennon let me use his twelve-string Rickenbacker for 'The Wild Side of Life.' When we finished, I'd give it back to John. I could tell that it was all too much for him. I don't think they had any interest in what they were doing. No one could hear what they were playing, and it was like the bird house of a zoo, greatly amplified. When they'd finished, the police appeared, and they fled as fast as they could into limousines. They weren't enjoying that."

The Beatles didn't perform in Liverpool again until December 5, 1965, when they played two shows at the Liverpool Empire for what would be the last time. For both shows, forty thousand applications for tickets were received, so thirty-five thousand fans missed out.

The Beatles were not given the Freedom of the City of Liverpool (an honor equivalent to receiving the key to the city in the United States) until 1984, John Lennon receiving his posthumously. This coincided with the UK premiere of Paul McCartney's film, *Give My Regards to Broad Street*.

Opposite, top: The souvenir program for the northern premiere of *A Hard Day's Night*.
Opposite, below: The Odeon cinema in London Road, Liverpool. The following year Bob Dylan appeared there and the sign outside said, "2.30 *The Sound of Music*, 7.30 Bob Dylan."
Top: The Beatles toured the UK with the Tamla-Motown artist Mary Wells and appeared at the Liverpool Empire on November 8, 1964.
Left: The Beatles at Abbey Road in September 1964, during the recording of *Beatles For Sale*.

7 A LEGACY TO LIVERPOOL

"I love the way Paul includes his whole family in whatever he does. He invites his relatives to the shows in Liverpool, and because John's gone, he always includes us."

JULIA BAIRD, JOHN LENNON'S HALF-SISTER

"Don't talk to me about music. I could have been in the fucking Beatles."

TOMMY IN WILLY RUSSELL'S PLAY
BREEZEBLOCK PARK

Left: The Cavern Club was rebuilt in 1984. The front area of the club with the "original" stage and brick arches is exactly the same size as the old Cavern. Merseybeat group members signed the wall at the back of the stage. The rebuilt Cavern also has a larger stage and performance area at the rear of the club.

WITH A FEW EXCEPTIONS, MERSEYBEAT WAS PLAYED by quartets of young white males, playing lead, rhythm, and bass guitars with drums. Rory Storm, born in January 1938, was among the older performers. Most groups had more than one lead singer and encouraged harmonies on love songs or exhortations to dance. They were mostly taken from obscure black American rhythm and blues records, although the repertoires did contain surprises—for example, "Over the Rainbow" (Beatles), "Easter Bonnet" (Swinging Blue Jeans), and "You'll Never Walk Alone" (Gerry and the Pacemakers)—which in 1963 became a number-one record and a football anthem.

By 1964, the key acts had moved away from Liverpool, and the bands that were performing in the clubs had not had national hits (Karl Terry and the Cruisers, Earl Preston and the Realms) or were the new generation (the Escorts, the Hideaways, the Clayton Squares). It was a bit like staging *Hamlet* without the Prince: the principal players were missing.

The Cavern's doorman, Paddy Delaney, found he had a new role. "Tourists were coming to Mathew Street and photographing the doorway. I had to stand on the door with people from all over the world asking me questions. One American girl wanted to see the band room. I pointed to where Ringo Starr always sat. She got down on her knees, and she kissed the spot and then broke down crying. There were scenes like that every day of the week."

Rather than follow his brother into a beat group, Mike McCartney chose to be part of a comedy-and-music act known as Scaffold, calling himself Mike McGear and appearing with John Gorman (a post office engineer) and Roger McGough (a teacher). The name came from a French film *Ascenseur pour l'échafaud* (Lift to the Scaffold), thereby revealing more esoteric tastes than the beat groups. They were still based in Liverpool, and each year they would create a new comedy and music revue for the Edinburgh Festival and for the Everyman Theatre in Hope Street, Liverpool.

Above, left: Cavern doorman Paddy Delaney standing outside the club. Today, this photograph can be seen next to the Cavern's original entrance.
Above, center: Scaffold with actress Sheila Fearn, known for playing Terry's sister in BBC-TV's *The Likely Lads*.
Above, right: The Clayton Squares with Mike Evans on the right.
Opposite, left: The Ramones outside Eric's.
Opposite, right: Tickets and a Special Members' card to Eric's, for Press and VIPs.

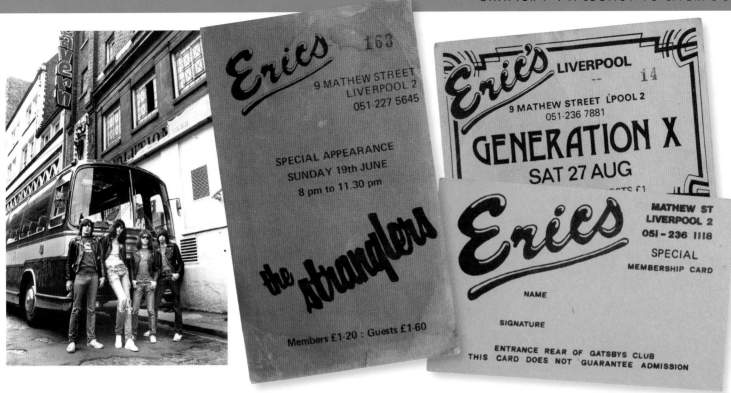

When the 1960s *Batman* TV series was at its height, Scaffold thought they had a winning satire with "Goodbat Nightman." "We went to Brian in his NEMS emporium," says Mike, "and said, 'We've got this crazy idea, but we've got to do it now.' He hemmed and hawed and wanted us to do other things. It didn't come out until the end of *Batman* mayhem, so the record didn't reach the audience it should have done, and I blame Brian Epstein for the failure of that record."

Moving to a theatrical agency in London, Scaffold had hits with "Thank U Very Much" (written after Paul had given Mike a Nikon camera) and "Lily the Pink" (a rugby song with cleaned-up lyrics). Prime Minster Harold Wilson said "Thank U Very Much" was his favorite song, but they incurred his wrath by writing and performing the sardonic *Yesterday's Men* for a BBC-TV documentary after the Labour Party lost the 1970 election.

Although the Beatles embraced psychedelia (another example of art school leanings) in 1967, most of the Liverpool bands were too grounded in reality to follow them. The thought of Gerry Marsden going psychedelic is preposterous, and the same can be said of the fashionable blues-based rock. Instead, several of the Liverpool bands

reverted to type and became stars on the cabaret circuit—that is, in the "chicken in a basket" northern clubs. Freddie Starr became a leading comic, while Cilla Black developed into a much-loved family entertainer.

The control of the music business had passed back to London, so Liverpool had become an anachronism. Mike Evans recalls Rory Storm making a guest appearance with the Clayton Squares. He asked Rory how he wanted to be introduced. "Just tell them the golden boy is here," said Rory.

The Beatles broke up in 1970 and all four musicians had successful solo careers. A backlash against the Beatles was noticeable among new musicians in Liverpool and elsewhere, largely because their heritage was too much to contemplate: how could any band emulate what they had accomplished?

In 1976, punk had a Year Zero stance whereby the past was supposedly ignored. On the B-side of their debut single, "1977," the Clash sang, "No Beatles, Elvis, or the Rolling Stones." Glen Matlock was allegedly fired by the Sex Pistols for talking about the Beatles. It was a pose, as several new wave musicians were to acknowledge their influence and cover their songs. In an interview, Paul Weller's mother went

Left: Andy McCluskey and Paul Humphreys founded British synthpop band Orchestral Manoeuvres in the Dark (OMD) in 1978. Originally from the Wirral Peninsula, here (l-r) bassist Andy McCluskey, drummer Malcolm Holmes, and keyboard player Paul Humphreys pose for a portrait next to Liverpool's ferry terminal, Pier Head, in 1982. Andy also created the girl group Atomic Kitten and wrote their number one hit, "Whole Again."

Below: Pete Wylie is known as the mouth of the Mersey, a musician with an informed opinion on any subject. He has had his success through bands with the word Wah! in their names (for example, the Mighty Wah!). He signs autographs "love and wah!" or "wah! and kisses" and he lives in a house called Disgraceland. His next album is to be titled *Pete Sounds.*

off-message to reveal how her son had collected the monthly *Beatles Book*.

This supposed aversion to the Beatles was accentuated in Liverpool. Most bands were determined not to sound like the Beatles and didn't want to acknowledge their influence. After all, how could a new band become the best act in the UK when it was impossible to be the best band from their home city?

Then it changed. In the 1980s, Liverpool musicians such as Pete Wylie and Ian McNabb were quick to praise the Beatles, and bands such as OMD, Echo and the Bunnymen, and the Farm promoted the city. Ian McNabb of the Icicle Works says, "When I started in 1975, the Beatles were a curse, as their shadow was just too huge. If you tried to get a record deal, the companies would say, 'Oh, Beatles,' which killed it. Then towards the end of the '70s, you had successful bands from Liverpool, like Wah! Heat, Echo and the Bunnymen, and the Teardrop Explodes. It destroyed the Beatles comparison, as most of the Liverpool bands sounded like they came from Los Angeles or New York. The musicians didn't speak too much about the Beatles in the '80s. Then Oasis came along, and that introduced a new generation into the music, and now you can't move for Beatles."

Successful musical acts have continued to come from Liverpool: in recent years, Atomic Kitten, the Coral, the Zutons, and the Wombats. A successful exhibition at the World Museum in 2008 was entitled *The Beat Goes On.* That still applies to the Merseysippi Jazz Band, who host a weekly residency, a role they have been performing, almost nonstop, since their formation in 1949.

THE MUSEUM OF LIVERPOOL

The Museum of Liverpool is part of National Museums Liverpool, which comprises Walker Art Gallery, World Museum, Merseyside Maritime Museum, International Slavery Museum, Sudley House, and the Lady Lever Art Gallery.

Opened in July 2011, the lavish museum, located on the waterfront, houses six thousand objects ranging in size from a Cavern membership card to a reconstruction of Pier Head station, where you can experience the world's first overhead electric railway. The museum covers the city's beginnings as a global city, its development in the Industrial Revolution, archaeological finds, and the voices of Liverpool from the last two hundred years. No visitor can fail to be impressed by the sheer number of familiar places and personalities associated with the city, and its influence on British culture in all its forms.

One of the main galleries, Wondrous Place, relates to Liverpool's artistic and sporting achievements. The *Liverpool Sound* exhibition features the St. Peter's church hall stage in front of which John Lennon first met Paul McCartney in 1957. Although there are plenty of Beatles exhibits, they form part of a wider Merseybeat story and history of Liverpool's entertainment and culture.

The memorabilia includes a 1959 bright yellow stage jacket from the Rockin' Cruisers, Billy Fury's first guitar, one of Lita Roza's dresses, and numerous tickets and posters. There are also temporary exhibitions: *Mike McCartney's Liverpool* exhibition was the first to be shown in the Skylight Gallery, featuring a stunning photograph of Brian Epstein. Although a new exhibition has now taken its place, some of Mike's photographs showing a selection of insights on his home city, are still on display in the museum.

The building is a fine addition to Liverpool's waterfront, and there are spectacular views over the Mersey through the twenty-four-meter-wide window. As most museums and art galleries cut out the light, this is a spectacular achievement.

Entry to the Museum of Liverpool is free. It is open from 10am-5pm seven days a week.

Above: The Wondrous Place gallery (named after a Billy Fury song) features memorabilia from sixty years of rock; center: the remarkable staircase; bottom: an external view of the Museum, which has been likened to a huge Polaroid camera.

BEATLES TOURISM

Every August holiday weekend, Liverpool becomes the tribute band capital of the world, as the Cavern City Tours' Beatles Convention gains in popularity and attracts star guests— Pete Best, Denny Laine, Tony Sheridan, and others from the Beatles' past.

However, every night in Liverpool there are acts singing Beatles' songs in clubs and bars. Nearly every touring musician includes a Beatles song or medley when performing in the city—even Bob Dylan sang George Harrison's "Something" at the Echo Arena in 2009.

There is much for Beatles' fans to see in Liverpool. The Cavern is, unarguably, the most famous club in the world. Nowadays anyone who saw the Beatles at the Cavern would have to be at least sixty-five years old, and it will be fascinating to see what happens when all of the Beatles' contemporaries have moved on.

The Beatles Story at the Albert Dock is one of the UK's top tourist attractions. In 2009, it held the *White Feather: The Spirit of Lennon* exhibition by Julian and Cynthia Lennon. The current temporary exhibition is *Elvis and Us*. Alongside Graceland memorabilia, it explores Elvis's influence on the Beatles and the group's first meeting with the King of Rock 'n' Roll in 1965.

Visitors can explore the National Trust–owned properties— Mendips, 251 Menlove Avenue, Woolton, and 20 Forthlin Road, Allerton—the childhood homes of John Lennon and Paul McCartney respectively. In 2012 the two properties were preserved by English Heritage as Grade II listed buildings. The National Trust has no plans to expand their portfolio to George's or Ringo's properties. There are also four streets in the Kensington area of Liverpool that have been named after the Beatles: John Lennon Drive, Paul McCartney Way, George Harrison Close, and Ringo Starr Drive. They were joined in 2011 by Pete Best Close, an apt address for the nearly Beatle.

But Liverpool is not just about old music. The Cavern, the Picket, Eric's, and many other clubs are keen to promote new sounds. The Liverpool Institute for Performing Arts (LIPA), founded by Paul McCartney in the premises of his old school, brings many fledgling singers and songwriters to the city, and they are often heard in the clubs and bars, not to mention LIPA's own festivals.

Left: The Beatles-themed hotel Hard Days Night on North John Street.
Opposite, left to right: The Beatles Story at the Albert Dock; you can sit at the same table as the Beatles at the Grapes pub on Mathew Street; Cavern Walks shopping centre; the Wondrous Place Gallery at the Museum of Liverpool.

Above: The Cavern Club, Mathew Street.
Left: Sculpture of Eleanor Rigby in Stanley Street.
Below: Liverpool singer and student Rachael Wright performing at LIPA's "3rd Degree" music festival.

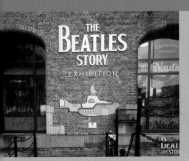

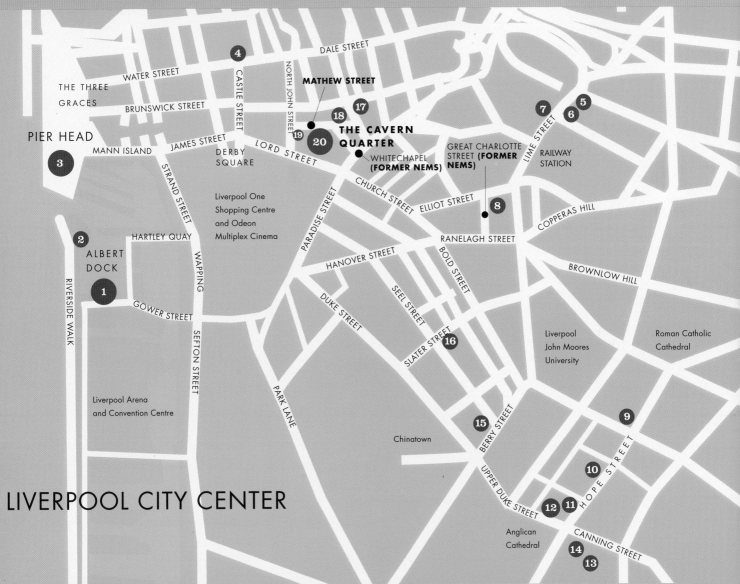

LIVERPOOL CITY CENTER

DALE STREET

WATER STREET

THE THREE
GRACES

BRUNSWICK STREET

CASTLE STREET

NORTH JOHN STREET

MATHEW STREET

PIER HEAD

MANN ISLAND

JAMES STREET

DERBY
SQUARE

LORD STREET

**THE CAVERN
QUARTER**

WHITECHAPEL
(FORMER NEMS)

GREAT CHARLOTTE
STREET (FORMER
NEMS)

LIME STREET

RAILWAY
STATION

STRAND STREET

Liverpool One
Shopping Centre
and Odeon
Multiplex Cinema

PARADISE STREET

CHURCH STREET

ELLIOT STREET

COPPERAS HILL

HARTLEY QUAY

ALBERT
DOCK

WAPING

RIVERSIDE WALK

GOWER STREET

SEFTON STREET

HANOVER STREET

RANELAGH STREET

BOLD STREET

BROWNLOW HILL

DUKE STREET

SEEL STREET

SLATER STREET

Liverpool
John Moores
University

Roman Catholic
Cathedral

PARK LANE

Liverpool Arena
and Convention Centre

Chinatown

BERRY STREET

HOPE STREET

UPPER DUKE STREET

Anglican
Cathedral

CANNING STREET

01 The Beatles Story	06 Empire Theatre	11 Former College of Art	16 Jacaranda Club
02 Tate Liverpool	07 St. George's Hall	12 LIPA	17 Eleanor Rigby Bronze
03 Museum of Liverpool	08 Former Blackler's Store	13 7 Percy Street	18 The Grapes pub
04 Liverpool Town Hall	09 Philharmonic pub	14 3 Gambier Terrace	19 Hard Days Night Hotel
05 Former Odeon Cinema	10 Ye Cracke pub	15 Blue Angel Club	20 The Cavern

Above: Gates to Strawberry Field. **Left:** The Empress, at the end of Ringo's street. **Below, left:** Flyer for the dance at Barnston Women's Institute on March 24, 1962. It was at this performance that the Beatles first wore suits. **Below, right:** Shops along Penny Lane, 1971. **Bottom:** Penny Lane today. **Opposite:** Top, Paul's house at 20 Forthlin Road; below, John's house at 251 Menlove Avenue.

The HESWALL JAZZ CLUB

present their

★ ALL ★ STAR ★ BILL

Starring

THE BEATLES

★ Mersey Beat Poll Winners!
★ Polydor Recording Artists!
★ Prior to European Tour!

★ plus

The Pasadena Jazzmen

Firm Favourites!

plus ★

'Top Twenty' Records

at Barnston Women's Institute
on Saturday March 24th, 1962
7-30 p.m. — 11-15 p.m.

7/6   ADMISSION   7
Strictly by TICKETS ONLY

F. W. COOPER SEAVIEW PRESS, 98, BOROUGH ROAD, BIRKENHEAD.

Tower Ballroom, New Brighton

NEW BRIGHTON

WALLASEY

Grosvenor Ballroom, Liscard

BIRKENHEAD

THE WIRRAL

Barnston Women's Institute, Heswall

HESWALL

Litherland Town Hall

Lathom Hall

WALTON

Clubmoor Conservative Club

ANFIELD

The Casbah

WEST DERBY
VILLAGE

EVERTON

KNOTTY ASH

The Grafton and Locarno

Mersey Tunnel

LIVERPOOL

TOXTETH

12 Arnold Grove

10 Admiral Grove

Rosebery Street

9 Newcastle Road

Penny Lane

Majestic Ballroom, Birkenhead

Empress Pub

9 Madryn Street

Quarry Bank School

Dovedale Primary

Strawberry Field

Mendips

20 Forthlin Road

St Peter's Church

WOOLTON

ALLERTON

RIVER

GARSTON

Hulme Hall, Port Sunlight

MERSEY

25 Upton Green

SPEKE

12 Ardwick Road

ESTUARY

LIVERPOOL'S
OUTLYING DISTRICTS

LIVERPOOL
JOHN LENNON AIRPORT

ACKNOWLEDGMENTS

The author and publishers would like to thank the following people for their assistance in producing this book:

Paul Gallagher and Janet Dugdale at National Museums Liverpool; Kevin Roach and Roger Hull at Liverpool Records Office; Cathy Elwin and Ken Clark at the New Brighton Heritage and Information Centre; Stephen Bailey; Tony Booth; Billy Butler; David Bedford; Rod Davis; Graham Duffy; Dave Forshaw; Colin and Sylvia Hall; Mark Lewisohn; Catherine Marcangeli; and Rod Murray. With special thanks to Mike Evans and Mark Naboshek for their advice and contribution, and for Mark's introduction to Ian James and Michael Hill. With the exception of the Beatles, all quoted interviews were conducted by the author, often for BBC Radio Merseyside. Thank you to all concerned.

BIBLIOGRAPHY

Many books have been consulted while writing this book, including the following: **Liddypool: Birthplace of the Beatles** David Bedford (Dalton Watson, 2009) | **Stuart Sutcliffe: A Retrospective** Matthew H. Clough, & Colin Fallows (Eds.)(Victoria Gallery & Museum, University of Liverpool, 2008) | **Brian Epstein** Ray Coleman (Viking, 1989) | **Beatle Pete, Time Traveller** Mallory Curley (Randy, 2005) | **The Beatles** Hunter Davies (Ebury, 2009) Updated version of 1968 biography | **The Quarrymen** Hunter Davies (Omnibus 2001) | **A Cellarful of Noise** Brian Epstein (Souvenir, 1964) | **The Beatles and Some Other Guys: Rock Family Trees of the Early Sixties** Pete Frame (Omnibus, 1997) | **The Beatles: From Cavern to Star-Club** Hans Olof Gottfridsson (Premium, 1997) | **Mersey Beat: The Beginning of the Beatles** Bill Harry (Omnibus, 1977) | **Never a Yes Man: The Life and Politics of an Adopted Liverpudlian** Eric Heffer (Verso, 1991) | **The Beatles Live!** Mark Lewisohn (Pavilion, 1986) | **The Lennon Companion** Liz Thomson & David Gutman (Eds.) (Macmillan, 1987)

PHOTO CREDITS